From Coins to Kings

FROM COINS TO KINGS

Daisy M. Jones

and

J. Louis Cooper

*The Harper & Row
Basic Reading Program*

*How to Read in the
Subject-Matter Areas*

Harper & Row, Publishers

*Evanston, Illinois   Elmsford, New York
Pleasanton, California   New York, New York*

Acknowledgments

The following acknowledgments are for the use of materials quoted or adapted. Notations in parentheses are references to this book—*From Coins to Kings*.

Doubleday & Company, Inc., for "What Is White?" from *Hailstones and Halibut Bones* by Mary O'Neill; copyright © 1961 by Mary Gibbons O'Neill. Reprinted by permission of Doubleday & Company, Inc. (Pages 211–212)

Doubleday & Company, Inc., for "Taxis," from *Taxis and Toadstools* by Rachel Field; copyright 1926 by Doubleday & Company, Inc. Reprinted by permission of the publisher. (Page 222)

Grosset & Dunlap, Inc., for adaptation of pages 7 and 11–17 from *Illustrated Book of Knights* by Jack Coggins; copyright © 1957 by Grosset & Dunlap, Inc. Used by permission of the publisher. (Pages 340–344)

Holt, Rinehart and Winston, Inc., for "To Beachey, 1912," from *Chicago Poems* by Carl Sandburg; copyright 1916 by Holt, Rinehart and Winston, Inc.; copyright renewed 1944 by Carl Sandburg. Reprinted by permission of Holt, Rinehart and Winston, Inc. (Pages 230–231)

Houghton Mifflin Company, for "Sea Shell," from *A Dome of Many-Colored Glass* by Amy Lowell; copyright 1940 by Ada Dwyer Russell. Used by permission of the publisher, Houghton Mifflin Company. (Page 234)

The Macmillan Company, for a portion of "The Ghost of the Buffaloes," by Vachel Lindsay, from *The Collected Poems of Vachel Lindsay;* copyright 1913, 1914, 1916, 1917, 1919, 1920, 1923, and 1925, by The Macmillan Company. Reprinted with permission of the publisher. (Page 213)

G. P. Putnam's Sons, for adaptation of pages 166–174 from *Seven Miles Down* by Jacques Piccard & Robert S. Dietz; © 1961 by Jacques Piccard & Robert S. Dietz. Used by permission of G. P. Putnam's Sons. (Pages 185–189)

Charles Scribner's Sons, for adaptation of portions from *How I Found Livingstone* by Henry M. Stanley; copyright 1913 by Charles Scribner's Sons. Used by permission of the publisher. (Pages 163–167)

Harper & Row, Publishers, Incorporated, for adaptation of pages 315–318 from *The Living Sea* by Captain J.-Y. Cousteau with James Dugan; copyright © 1963 by Harper & Row, Publishers, Incorporated. (Pages 190–194)

Harper & Row, Publishers, Incorporated, for quotations from *The House of Sixty Fathers* by Meindert DeJong, copyright © 1956 by Meindert DeJong; from *New York to Rome: Jet Flight 808* by Leonard A. Stevens, copyright © 1962 by Leonard A. Stevens; from *Charlotte's Web* by E. B. White, copyright 1952 by E. B. White; and from *Farmer Boy* by Laura Ingalls Wilder, copyright 1933 by Harper & Brothers. Used with permission of Harper & Row, Publishers, Incorporated. (Pages 218–219; 14–15; 216–217; and 222–223)

Illustrations by:

James Curran
Paul Hazelrigg
John Langston
H. Charles McBarron

Charles Moser
Tak Murakami
Jo Anna Poehlmann
George Roth

Photographs

Courtesy of Abbott Laboratories, page 295
Courtesy of the American Museum of Natural History, page 317 bottom photo
Courtesy of the Art Institute of Chicago, page 323
The Bettmann Archive, map on page 120
Source material for artist's illustrations of explorers in Unit Three, The Bettmann Archive and Brown Brothers
Courtesy of the Corning Glass Works, page 275
Courtesy of Eastman Kodak, page 317 two upper right-hand photos
Freelance Photographers Guild, page 318
Harold V. Green, pages 286 and 287
Courtesy of Mount Wilson and Palomar Observatories, pages 303, 306 left, 309, and 310
John Ott Pictures, Incorporated, page 321
Rapho-Guillumette, page 319
Courtesy U.S. Coast and Geodetic Survey, page 317 upper left-hand photo
Courtesy Yerkes Observatory, page 306 right

CONTENTS

UNIT ONE

How to Improve Your Reading

Most people read something every day. How is reading used in the illustrations below?

Can you think of other times when people need to read?

AN OVERVIEW
OF GOOD READING HABITS

A good reader always wants to become a better reader. Your reading will improve as you follow these rules for better reading.

1. KEEP YOUR MIND ON WHAT YOU ARE READING.

2. KNOW WHY YOU READ.

3. KNOW THE MEANING AND THE PRONUNCIATION OF EVERY WORD.

4. FIT YOUR SPEED TO YOUR NEEDS.

5. KNOW WHAT YOU READ.

6. READ TO UNDERSTAND RELATIONSHIPS.

7. BUILD MENTAL IMAGES AS YOU READ.

8. RECOGNIZE IMPORTANT DETAILS.

9. LOCATE INFORMATION OUTSIDE YOUR TEXT.

Let's take a quick look at examples of these rules. You will learn some ways to use the rules to improve your reading. In this book you will find many helps in the material printed on blue paper. You CAN improve your reading!

KEEP YOUR MIND ON WHAT
YOU ARE READING

When you KEEP YOUR MIND ON WHAT YOU ARE READING, you are CONCENTRATING. You are able to remember more of what you have read when you CONCENTRATE.

CONCENTRATE as you read the following paragraphs. Do not let anything disturb you. Discover how much you can remember.

The jet pilot walked out of the terminal building directly to the MATS Mule's left landing gear and began looking at the four large tires. The captain circled around the gear and ducked under the plane's belly to the other main gear below the great swept-back wing. Next he went back to the

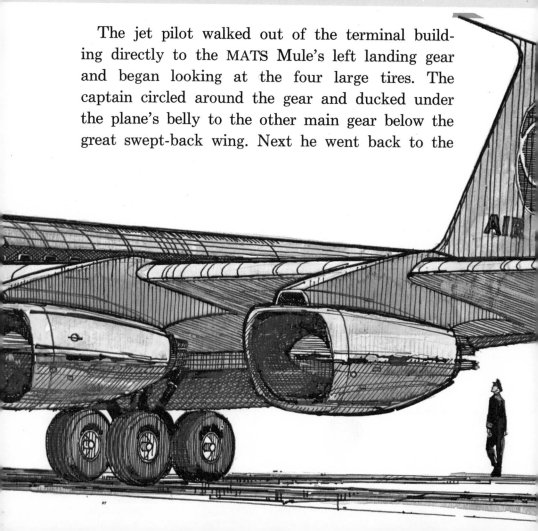

jet's tail and looked up and around the towering vertical fin, three or four stories high. Kratovil then walked the length of the airplane and checked the nose wheel. From there the captain stepped to the front portable stairway and walked briskly up into the big jet air liner.

"I never like to take off in any kind of an airplane," he once said, "unless I first have a good look at it. It's a habit that I've stuck to for years. I started doing it back when I first commenced flying and I still do. Maintenance does a tremendous job these days, but I don't feel right until I've looked for myself."

1. Did you CONCENTRATE?
2. What parts of the jet were inspected?
3. How do you know it was a large plane?
4. Why did the pilot inspect the outside of the jet?
5. Why do you think Captain Kratovil was a good pilot?

KNOW WHY YOU READ

When you KNOW WHY YOU READ, you have A PURPOSE FOR READING. Many things can give you this purpose. Some of them are: (1) illustrations, (2) titles of stories or books, and (3) study guides.

Is there anything in this illustration which makes you curious? Do you want to find out something about it? If so, the illustration gives you A PURPOSE FOR READING.

THE MYSTERY
OF THE
STOLEN IDOL

Read this title. Does it make you want to read the story?

Be ready to discuss how
the lives of the people of India
are affected by —
1. The size of the population
2. The climate
3. The geography

When you see a study guide on the chalkboard, what is your PURPOSE FOR READING? Can you name other things which give you a PURPOSE FOR READING?

KNOW THE MEANING AND THE PRONUNCIATION OF EVERY WORD

Many of the words we use can have several, or multiple, meanings. In the sentence, "*The accident was a bit of hard luck,*" what does the word "hard" mean? Study the illustrations and phrases which follow. Make as many sentences as you can in which the word "hard" has a different meaning.

hard work
hard-hearted
hard cash
hard and fast rule
hard as nails

A large number of our English words were taken from other languages. When you know the origin of the root word and its original meaning, you will often have a better understanding of many English words which have the same root.

The seven words below come from the Latin root *pend* meaning "hang." Can you find the idea of "hanging" in each word? Do you need to know something about prefixes and suffixes to get the complete meaning?

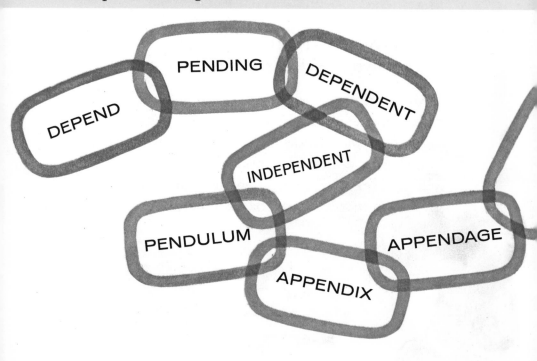

DEPEND

PENDING

DEPENDENT

INDEPENDENT

PENDULUM

APPENDIX

APPENDAGE

Often, but not always, the way a word is used in the sentence will give you a clue to its meaning. What is the meaning of each underlined word as used in the following sentences? Use context clues.

1. While the English dawdled, the Americans hurried to the attack.

2. Tom gets along with so many people because he is so diplomatic.

3. The loud thunder and sharp lightning made the dog cringe in fear.

4. He had had so much trouble that he was used to adversity.

5. The streets were being repaired on the south side of town. The high school was having a parade before the football game. These things and the narrow streets on the north side all helped to impede the traffic.

6. Jim ran the race in record time, and the coach is going to record it in the school track book.

You have used multiple meanings, knowledge of root words, prefixes, and suffixes, and context clues to help you decide the meaning and pronunciation of many words on these pages. Now check your thinking with the Glossary and the dictionary.

FIT YOUR SPEED TO YOUR NEEDS

Some reading material can and should be read rapidly. Other materials need to be read slowly. It is a wise reader who learns to fit his reading speed to his needs.

Read the titles of the following selections. Do the titles suggest your speed of reading? What speed will you use for the first selection? the second selection?

Do an Experiment

You will need a nickel, a water glass, and a thin smooth card, large enough to cover the glass.

Rest the card on the tumbler and put the coin in the center of the card. With the middle finger of your right hand, shoot the card off the tumbler.

What happens to the coin?

The Last of the Ninth

It was the last of the ninth inning. Two men were out and the bases were full. The visiting team was ahead 5 to 2. Tex had three balls and two strikes against him. This next pitch could mean the game! Tex tapped his shoes and took his position. The pitcher stretched and let fly a fast ball. Crack—the ball sailed out and over the fence. A mighty roar went up from the crowd—the home team had won its first game.

Why did you use different speeds of reading?
Did you find that the titles of the selections suggested your speed of reading?

KNOW WHAT YOU READ

CONCENTRATE as you read this summary of a
news article which tells how men lived in Antarctica during the winter of 1963.

Life in Antarctica

About 300 Americans lived in stations in Antarctica during the winter [our spring and summer] of
1963. Because buildings on the surface had often
been crushed by the weight of the snow, this new
station had buildings built in tunnels. To make the
tunnels, trenches were first dug by huge snowplows.
When the trenches were deep enough, curved sections of steel were placed as roofs over their tops.
The steel sections were used as forms on which to
blow specially treated snow. In a few days, the
snow was as hard as rock.

Many of the men could do their work without
ever going to the surface. In the tunnels they had
means for making electric power. They had a hospital, laboratories for scientists, and garages where
men worked on equipment. There were sleeping
quarters, and the dining rooms were painted in

bright, cheerful colors. Some of the buildings had offices. Everything possible was provided to make life easier for the men who are living and working in Antarctica.

Now close your book. How many facts from "Life in Antarctica" can you remember?

Reread the summary and take brief notes as you read. Close your book again and cover your notes. How many facts can you remember this time?

Organizing your facts in an outline will help you KNOW WHAT YOU READ. Fill in an outline under the following main heads, using as many subheads as you need to cover the facts:

    I. How the tunnels are built
    II. What the buildings contain

Reading, rereading, taking notes, and *outlining* help you KNOW WHAT YOU READ.

READ TO UNDERSTAND RELATIONSHIPS

Study the graph below and the following paragraph. Do you see any relationship between them?

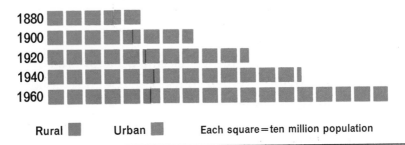

RURAL AND URBAN POPULATION OF THE UNITED STATES 1880-1960

Rural ■   Urban ■   Each square=ten million population

"Things have changed since my father's day," Grandfather said as he looked at the graph in Tom's social studies book. "When he was young there was wood to cut, water to carry, butter to make, and gardens to plow. There were lamps to fill, cows to milk, bread to bake, and horses to feed. There were errands to run, stoves to clean, potatoes to dig, and leaves to rake. Young people had plenty to do in those days."

Use the information from the graph and paragraph and discuss these questions.

1. About how many people lived in rural areas in 1880? in 1960?

2. Why do most of the chores listed in Grandfather's conversation differ from your chores today?

3. Which of the chores listed would you do today?

4. About how many people lived in urban areas in 1880? in 1960?

5. What do you think caused the shift from rural to urban living?

6. How has this shift changed the lives of many people?

Which of the six questions can be answered from the facts given? Which ones can be discussed if you understand relationships?

BUILD MENTAL IMAGES AS YOU READ

As you read this paragraph, try to build mental images of, or VISUALIZE, everything in the selection that follows.

Jim's Discovery

The trail-building was hard work and the canyon was very hot. "That's enough work for today, men," said Slim as he mopped his face. "Jim, you can go exploring if you wish, but keep your eyes and ears open for rattlers."

"I'm going to explore that steep canyon over to the left," called Jim as he raced away from the work camp.

Soon he had to slow down because there was no trail. He had to pull himself over sharp boulders taller than himself and edge along the narrow ledges at the side of the canyon. An eagle drifted above him in the bright blue of the sky. Jim's ears were intent for the rattle of a snake. He carried a stick and stirred it about on the rocks above him before putting his hands in any place which he could not see. Luck was with him and no stir of a snake answered him from above.

Finally Jim reached the top of the canyon and dropped exhausted on a flat boulder. He closed his eyes for a moment, but a strange sound made him go to the other side of the boulder.

There he stopped in surprise, for below him was a small waterfall. It seemed impossible in this arid, rocky spot. Jim felt all the joy of an explorer. He had discovered treasure—the treasure of cool, clear water in this hot, dry place.

Discuss your mental images with your classmates. Don't be surprised if all of you do not have the same mental images. The same words can build different mental images for different people. Learning to VISUALIZE will help you become a better reader.

RECOGNIZE IMPORTANT DETAILS

Study the illustrations of the clown and the magician. How are the two costumes alike? How are they different? Telling how things are alike or different is one way to RECOGNIZE IMPORTANT DETAILS.

Now see if you can RECOGNIZE IMPORTANT DETAILS in the following selection.

"Jack, will you please get this costume for me at the rental store?" asked Ned, as he handed Jack this slip of paper.

RENT A COSTUME

It is black and red with large pockets.
The large sleeves may hide many things.
The hat is a special type of hat.
If I wore the costume on the street, people
  might laugh.
I will wear it on a stage and will enter-
  tain people.
My main purpose is to make people laugh.
Which costume do I want?

Jack read the paper and with a puzzled look on his face said, "Didn't you give me the wrong paper?"

"No," said Ned, smiling. "If you will read the riddle carefully and watch for details, you will know which costume to rent."

Pretend you are Jack. Do you know which costume to rent? You may want to reread the selection. Which details in the riddle were true of both costumes? What was the important detail which gave you the answer to the riddle?

LOCATE INFORMATION
OUTSIDE YOUR TEXT

ENCYCLOPEDIA

TABLE OF CONTENTS

DICTIONARY

LIBRARY
CARD
CATALOGUE

MAP

INDEX

BIOGRAPHY

Some Sources of Information

Seven sources of information are pictured above
What other sources can you name?

Many libraries have a *Reader's Guide,* which helps
you locate magazine articles about information you
need.

From the sources pictured, where will you look for:

1. The best route from Los Angeles to New York?
2. A list of stories in a book?
3. The definition of a word?
4. The events in a person's life?
5. The main industries of France?
6. Books about ants?
7. An experiment on air pressure in your science book?

When you use some of the sources pictured above, you will need to know the alphabet. Which sources are they?

Learning to LOCATE INFORMATION OUTSIDE YOUR TEXT will help you become a better reader.

You have reviewed the BETTER READING RULES to help you to become a better reader. Now, as you read the rest of this book, you will see how these rules apply to different kinds of reading materials.

Reading for Recreation

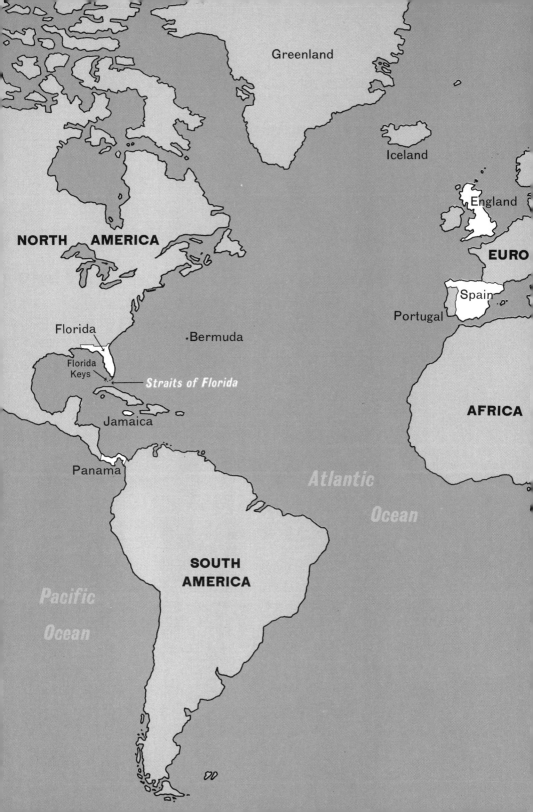

THE MYSTERY OF THE GOLD COINS

The above title tells what the next unit of this book is about. If you like mystery stories, as many people do, the title will give you a PURPOSE FOR READING, and will make it easy for you to CONCENTRATE.

Your speed will probably be fast because you will want to find out what the mystery is.

Before you start to read, you will want to locate these places mentioned in the story:

Florida   Spain   The Florida Keys
Panama   England   The Straits of Florida
Jamaica   Bermuda

CHAPTER I

A Narrow Escape

Allen could not breathe; his lungs were ready to burst! He tried so hard to wave at Tom, but his arms moved with frightening slowness. About twenty feet of ocean water pressed heavily on him. And for the first time since he had learned to scuba dive, he was afraid.

Even though Tom was almost close enough to touch, Allen in his panic was unable to reach him.

He tried to take another breath and gasped. He now knew that something was wrong with his aqualung. He waved again. Tom didn't see him. The

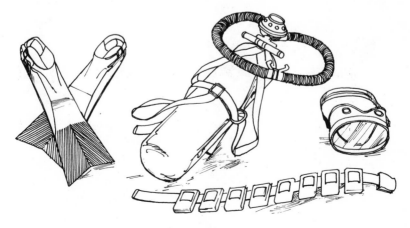

ocean which he had always thought of as a friend now seemed to be an enemy.

Allen tried to fight down his panic. He had been scuba diving for two years, but this was his first underwater trip off the Florida Keys. This part of the ocean's floor, with its pale coral cliffs, was unknown to him. The treacherous currents were driving him toward the sharp coral. He was suddenly afraid that the strong current he was in would sweep him behind a reef, sweep him forever beyond Tom's sight.

With one kick of his flippers, Tom went beyond reach. Even if he wanted to, Allen would not be able to touch him now. Allen's panic rose again. He fought it down. He remembered the way to reach the surface—kick slowly and breathe steadily. The air in his lungs would expand as the water pressure lessened. Allen's hand was on his belt, ready to release the weights that held him at this depth.

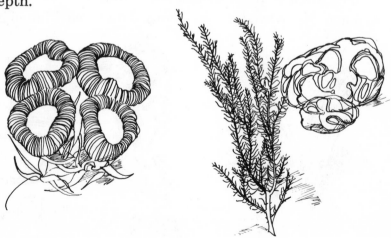

At that minute Tom reached the coral cave and turned to make sure that his partner was in sight. Allen would have sighed with relief, had his bursting lungs permitted. He drew his hand across his throat —the signal they had agreed upon—the signal that meant he was suffocating.

With a good strong kick, Tom was beside Allen, offering him the mouthpiece of the tube that led to his aqualung. They surfaced together, taking turns at breathing from Tom's air supply. Rising slowly, they gave their bodies time to become accustomed to the changing pressure of the water.

When Allen's head broke through the surface, he saw again the brilliant Florida sunlight. He shoved his mask up to his forehead and looked around for their boat.

There it was, barely thirty feet away, with Tom's sister, Louise, sitting in it calmly reading a book. Allen shot Tom a quick look of thanks as he gulped

in his first few lungfuls of fresh air. Then, after resting for a few minutes, they both struck out for the boat, swimming with long, even strokes.

"For a minute, I thought that was the end of me," Allen said to Tom.

When they got to the boat, Tom called to his sister, "Allen's coming first. Something happened to his air supply. He may need help."

The weight of the aqualung made Allen feel top-heavy. And the big flippers, as always, made it difficult to climb the ladder into the boat.

When he got into the boat, he unfastened the straps that held the aqualung. Breathing calmly now, he knew that the time without air had not harmed him. He put out his hand to help Tom into the boat.

"Before I put my gear away, I'm going to check the fittings on my aqualung. I must have adjusted it incorrectly. These lungs are practically fool-proof," Allen said. Then he looked straight at Tom and laughed, "I never thought I'd be so glad to see your funny-looking face. I really thought I'd taken my last breath before you turned around and saw me."

Tom grinned his crooked grin. "Running out of air is one thing you never have to worry about if I'm around," Tom assured him. "Any good scuba diver knows you should always keep your partner in sight."

"No more diving for Allen today, though," Tom's sister said. "He has to be sure he's all right before he goes down again."

"Oh, I feel fine," answered Allen. "But what about that picnic you brought along, Louise?"

Louise opened the picnic basket and neatly arranged napkins, hamburgers, carrots, and lemonade on the seat beside her. Watching her, it was hard for Allen to believe that he had met her and Tom only a few days ago. He had wasted the first few days of his Florida vacation feeling sorry that he had no friends here and wondering if he would ever get a chance to use his scuba diving equipment. He shouted with joy one day when his mother said at lunch, "I think I've found a partner for you, Allen. I met a lady today who has a son and a daughter about your age. They are coming over to meet you this evening. Her son wants to scuba dive, too."

For the last few days, the three friends had done everything together. Every day they drove their motorboat away from the crowded beaches, and Louise stayed in the boat while the boys explored underwater areas. Now they were the only swimmers near this isolated key.

"You know," Tom said, as he picked out a hamburger, "I think I was just coming on something interesting when your aqualung stopped working. It looked as if there was something in that cave

shaped like the hull of a big ship. I wonder if there could be sunken vessels around here. Didn't Spanish merchant ships sail through the Straits of Florida hundreds of years ago on their way to Spain from Spanish colonies in Latin America? What if one of the ships went aground on the coral reef and sank?"

"Yes, ships were sunk in these waters," Louise told her brother. "Spanish ships did sail near here and they were always in danger of being driven on the reefs during a storm. Pirates attacked them, too, and there was a time in history when English and Spanish ships were attacking each other. In that period many ships were sunk."

"And why couldn't one of those ships have been filled with gold?" asked Tom.

Louise laughed. "I may not be a diver," she said, "but I've learned a few things about the reefs and the animals that live in these waters from this book I've been reading. If a Spanish galleon sank near

here, you probably wouldn't see the whole hull today unless coral and limestone sealed it. Ships were made of wood in those days, and there's a worm, called the teredo, that lives in the water. Teredos eat wood." She smiled at her brother. "There may be gold down there, but the teredos could have eaten much of the boat."

"You're really learning something from that book, aren't you?" Allen said, with a new respect for Tom's pretty sister. "Did it tell you what we should look for if we want to find sunken treasure in these waters?"

Louise looked serious for a few seconds. Then she said, "Well, coral would have covered almost anything resting on the bottom of the ocean near these keys for more than a hundred years. But coral naturally grows in irregular shapes. If you come across coral in a roundish shape, for example, it might be that a man-made object would be inside it. If you happen to see a piece of coral like that, bring it up. After you chip away the coral, it might turn out to be something valuable."

Tom studied a piece of coral he had broken from the reef before Allen's trouble with the aqualung. Visions of gold coins and precious jewels raced through his mind. But his daydreaming was suddenly interrupted when Louise reminded him that it was time to start home.

USING WORDS TO DESCRIBE FEELINGS

Allen had many different experiences in Chapter I. These experiences led him to have feelings of: (1) fear, (2) relief, (3) confidence, (4) panic, and (5) curiosity.

Reread Chapter I and find the part in which Allen experienced these feelings. Read aloud the part that goes with each feeling. Now list the feelings in the sequence, or order, in which they come in the story.

OBSERVING AUTHOR'S WORD CHOICE

A good author chooses his words carefully. He wants to give you a good mental image of the events in his story. He uses exact words and colorful words.

These are examples of some of the phrases the author of our story used. See if you can say the same thing using different phrases.

fight down his panic

surfaced together

a Spanish galleon

this isolated key

went aground

the hull of a big ship

sighed with relief

a man-made object

Were your phrases or the author's phrases more exact or colorful? Why?

CHAPTER II

A Search for Treasure

If you expect something, you look forward to it or anticipate it. Find out what the boys are anticipating in Chapter II.

The next day the boys decided to look for sunken ships on the ocean floor. At first they left their aqualungs in the boat. In order to see a large area, they floated face down near the surface, using face masks and snorkels. It was easy to see through the clear water. They saw fish below them—black angelfish and swarms of small pink shrimp swimming backward.

Tom became curious about the mysterious caves in the reef at their right. He pointed to one and said, "Let's explore that cave before we forget where it is. We can look for treasure later."

Allen agreed. The boys climbed the ladder to the boat and strapped on their aqualungs. Allen carefully rechecked his fittings. He was not going to

repeat yesterday's mistake! Tom carried his spear gun when they descended. He loaded it in the water, carefully pointing it away from Allen and the boat.

They knew the dangers of caves to divers and never went far into deep ones. The cave Tom had chosen looked deep and dark at first. But after

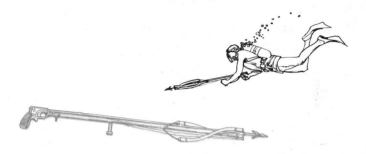

they swam into it for a few feet, their eyes adjusted to this dark green twilight world. They saw that the cave was only a few feet deep. Fish in many shapes and colors emerged from its crevices and swam past them, disturbed by the humans entering their homes. The water was cold and quiet in the cave; there were no currents like those that buffeted the reef outside. As Tom rested against a boulder, he turned to look back at the opening they had come through.

Suddenly he pointed through the opening. They were looking at the ocean floor strewn with coral-covered boulders in many shapes. Allen saw what Tom was pointing at—something flat and smooth shining in the green light. Could it be gold?

He headed toward it, gesturing for Tom to follow. They glided out of the mouth of the cave. Allen reached it first, but in a glance he saw that the shining object half-covered by sand was not gold. It was only a piece of window glass!

Through his mask Allen grinned at Tom, shrugged, and beckoned him on to explore another cave. But when he looked back, Tom was still hovering over the shining piece of glass. While Allen waited impatiently, Tom carefully picked up the piece of glass and fanned away the sand from the ocean floor below it. A close look at the ocean floor showed something gleaming between a crack in a small piece of coral. It was a coin!

Seeing Tom's discovery, Allen joined the search. As they swept through the sand, they found a piece of coral shaped like a dagger. Tom tried to hit it on a stone to break the coral, but the water cushioned the blow and the coral would not break.

Tom wedged his spear gun between the rocks so that the current could not carry it away. He took the dagger and coin from Allen and put them near the gun. They began sweeping through the sand again, adding all the small pieces of coral they found to their pile. With only an hour's supply of air in their tanks, they worked quickly and soon had so large a pile that each one had to make several trips, hands loaded with treasures, to the boat.

"We've found a shipwreck!" Allen told Louise when he surfaced for the first time. "Look at this coral!"

By the time it was all in the boat, Louise had chipped the coral from the coin by hitting it with a hammer.

"I think it must be Spanish," she cried, studying it closely. "Anyway, it isn't English. The date is worn off, so we can't find out anything about how old the shipwreck is. It may not be a shipwreck you've found," she added. "A small boat with only a few men aboard could have capsized here."

Tom and Allen, face masks on their foreheads, hands on the edge of the boat, stayed in the water while they debated. How would they mark the place where they had found the dagger and the coin so that they could find it again the next day?

"Let's use the inner tube we carry for emergencies," Allen suggested. "We can anchor it with a rope tied to a boulder at the bottom."

Tom tied one end of the rope on the inner tube. Meanwhile, Allen, still wearing his aqualung, took the other end and dived. Although his supply of air was getting low, he searched the ocean floor for a few minutes, looking for a boulder so shaped that the rope could be securely tied to it. After he found a long one, with thick coral growing upward at one end, he began to tie the rope to it. Then he looked again. No wonder he had selected this place to tie his rope. It wasn't a rock at all. It *was* a ship's anchor with one prong hidden in the sand, its iron disguised by centuries of coral crust!

Allen, his air nearly exhausted by now, surfaced slowly.

"That was no small boat we found, Tom," he said as soon as he could talk. "We found a real shipwreck. I tied the inner tube to a boulder which turned out to be a ship's anchor. It's a big one, too —much longer than I am tall."

Tom wanted to go down to see the anchor, but Louise reminded him that it was late afternoon. They should be starting home. So the three friends made plans for returning the next day to the isolated key and their underwater discovery.

"If we find more treasure tomorrow, we'll need something to carry it in from the ocean floor to the surface," Allen said. "It should be something that doesn't hold water. A net or a loosely woven basket would probably be best. I'll see what I can find tonight."

Tom said, "We want to be sure to keep our discovery secret, so we will mark the spot with the inner tube tonight only. We should find landmarks along the coast so that we can bring our boat to about the same place tomorrow. If we use landmarks instead of the inner tube, our secret will be safe. Once we get near the reef, we should be able to find this spot easily enough."

"You're right," said Allen, "and tonight I'll buy a grease pencil and plastic sheet that can be used for writing under water. Then tomorrow, we can make an underwater map, showing the caves in relation to the wreck."

Before they started the trip back, Tom drew a sketch of the beach near the reef. "Tomorrow we'll check this sketch carefully," said Allen.

REMEMBERING DETAILS

Even though you may have read Chapter II quickly, you probably remember quite a few details. How many of the following questions can you answer?

1. What happened when the boys' eyes adjusted to the dark green twilight world?
2. What equipment did the boys use?
3. What dangers were there on the ocean floor?
4. What things did the boys see on the ocean floor?
5. What are landmarks above the ocean surface?
6. What happens when a boat capsizes?

If you were unable to remember all of the details you needed to answer the questions, you will want to reread Chapter II.

Discussion

Discuss the next four questions. The answers may not be given in the chapter, but this will give you an opportunity to think and to draw some conclusions.

1. Why did the boys plan to return?
2. Why did Tom carry a spear gun?
3. Why did the boys use their face masks and snorkels before they went down to the cave area?
4. Why did the boys want to keep their discovery a secret?

Discuss how the choice of words in the next sentences help build mental images.

1. The treasure was disguised by centuries of coral crust.
2. The boys glided out of the cave.
3. The water cushioned the blow and the coral would not break.

Oral Reading

The feelings the boys had in this chapter can be divided into three parts: (1) adventure, (2) excitement, and (3) anticipation. Find and read aloud these three parts.

CHAPTER III

The Man with the Gray Beard

Meeting a stranger can make you feel any one of several different ways. He may be so friendly and pleasant that you trust him at once without really knowing much about him. He may be quiet or serious, causing you to wonder whether you dare to trust him or not. He may question you until you are not sure how much you should tell him.

In Chapter III a new character is introduced. As you read, you will discover how the boys feel about him. Why do they feel this way?

In this chapter, also, you will learn more about the characters of Tom, Allen, and Louise. Try reading this chapter with a pencil and note paper handy and jot down words which describe the four characters.

When they docked their boat, the boys agreed not to meet again until early the next morning. Therefore Allen was surprised, as he sat on the porch of his cottage that night, to see Tom hurry to his door.

"That sister of mine may have ruined all our plans," Tom said as soon as Allen opened the screen door. He sounded very angry with Louise and had difficulty in keeping his voice low. "You heard me say that we should keep the skipwreck a secret, didn't you?"

"Has she told someone about it?" Allen asked.

"A man with a gray beard lives in the cottage next to ours," Tom explained. "He speaks English with a heavy accent. Tonight after dinner, I heard Louise having a long conversation with him. Afterward I asked her what they were talking about, and she said that she showed him the coin that we found. She said she asked him if he could read the words on it. He kept asking her questions, and she ended up by telling him all about the discovery. I told her she couldn't come with us tomorrow if she can't keep a secret any better than that."

"Does she realize that the man may take our treasure?" Allen stormed.

"Oh, yes, she's very sorry about it—now that the damage is done," Tom answered angrily.

Allen thought for a moment or two and then he said, "Well, he probably won't go out looking for it tonight. Let's meet at the boat the first thing in the morning, as soon as the sun is up. Tell Louise she can come, but she's got to promise not to say another word about the secret treasure to anyone. When we get to the inner tube, we'll check the map of the beach that you made yesterday and make sure it's accurate. You can make your underwater map when we dive, and we'll bring up all the treasure we can tomorrow. Then, when we take the inner tube away, we'll have to rely on our maps."

"I don't think we should take Louise," Tom said. "What if the bearded man comes along in a boat and recognizes her? I don't think he'd recognize me, but after that conversation tonight, he'll never forget Louise."

"You know it isn't safe for us to dive without another person in a boat," Allen argued. "If the man with the accent comes along, Louise can signal to us to stay under water. If he asks what she is doing out there alone, she can always make up a good excuse."

Tom finally agreed, and by the time he left he was not quite so angry with Louise.

"By the way," Allen asked as Tom opened the door, "what did the man say about the coin?"

"He said it was Spanish and of small value when the ship sank. But I'll bet it's very valuable now because it's so old. He said the piece of glass was old, too. Did you notice how wavy it was?"

Long after he was in bed that night, Allen thought about their discovery. He was eager to bring to light those objects that had been on the bottom of the ocean for so long. He wondered if they would ever know the story of how the ship was wrecked. Where was it going? Where had it come from? And all night he dreamed of the bearded man who seemed so dangerously close to their treasure.

At sunrise the next morning, they set out in the boat. Tom still spoke curtly to his sister. He had not forgiven her for last night. And he looked back suspiciously, searching for the man with the gray beard until the dock was out of sight. However, at this early hour no one was on the dock and no other boat was in motion. When they reached the isolated key, Tom was in a better mood. They anchored the boat beside the inner tube and checked Tom's sketch of the beach. Two tall trees were selected as landmarks. The boys, eager to know if the treasure had been disturbed, strapped on their aqualungs and dived. They saw that the boulders apparently lay strewn as they had been for the last three centuries. Nothing had been touched since last night.

They had learned yesterday that it was hard to fan away the sand on the floor with their hands. Therefore, to make it easier, Tom had brought two small paddles. As soon as Allen had sketched

his underwater map, he joined Tom in looking for more coins. Lying face down near the ocean floor, they waved sand away with sweeping motions of the paddles. They searched systematically and soon came across more coins as well as another dagger.

They put the coral-encrusted coins in the basket and signaled for Louise to haul it to the surface. One hour of diving yielded enough treasure to cover the bottom of the small boat. Tom brought up a coral rock about nine inches in diameter. He suspected that a cannon ball might be beneath its coral cover. Near the surface, he beckoned Allen to help him put it in the boat. Allen climbed in the boat and bent over to lift the rock.

"See if you can help, Louise," he called after the coral rock almost slipped from his hands. But they found that with three of them tugging with all their might, they could not lift out of the water what one of them had been able to carry under water.

They gave up, afraid the boat would capsize with so much weight on one side of it. They let the rock fall back to the ocean floor.

"If it's that heavy, you must be right about its being a cannon ball," Allen said. "Only iron would weigh that much."

Later when they docked the boat, Tom said, "We'd better take the treasure to Allen's cottage. We've got to hide it from the bearded man."

They carried it in sacks, ignoring the curious glances of the people they met on the way. When they reached Allen's back porch, they spread the coral pieces on newspapers and began to chip away the rock-like coral. It was hard, exhausting work.

"Imagine cleaning the coral off that cannon ball!" Louise exclaimed after a few minutes of using a hammer on a coral-encrusted dagger.

"You'd need a sledge hammer," Allen agreed. "You know, Tom," he added, with his eyes shining, "if that boat carried cannon balls, it must have carried a cannon."

"If you boys plan to put a cannon in that little boat we've been using, you'll need a stronger helper than I," Louise said dryly. "Besides, you would need a larger boat."

"It would take a lot of money to hire the kind of equipment we'd need to haul most of that ship-wreck to the shore," Allen agreed.

"That's why I don't think Tom should be so angry with me for talking to the man next door," Louise said. "He seemed very much interested in shipwrecks, and he might be able to help you."

"He looks like a very suspicious character to me," Tom said. "He'd help us until he found out where the shipwreck is. Then he'd take all the treasure for himself. Remember, you promised not to talk to him any more."

Sitting on the floor of the porch, they worked at the treasure until it grew dark. They lowered their voices to excited whispers when Tom cracked the limestone from a golden coin. He made out the date, 1660, and passed it to Louise to see if she could read any of the letters. "Philippus," she read. "That's Latin for Philip. Then there are four capital I's. They represent the Roman numeral IV as we write it today. So it must mean Philip IV," she whispered. "Now we need to find out which country had a king named Philip IV in 1660."

Tom got Louise's book and looked it up. "Spain," he told them. "Philip IV was king there from 1621 to 1665. A ship from any country could have been carrying Spanish coins, of course, but at least we have a date to work on. The ship must have been sunk sometime in 1660 or later."

Louise said, "I think this coin must be a doubloon. Doubloons were Spanish golden coins whose worth varied from about five dollars to about sixteen dollars. They were the first things pirates looked for when they looted a ship."

They worked on, and the beach became silent. It was as if they were the only people for miles around. Except for the sound of the hammer tapping on the coral, they worked in a silence as deep and shadowy as the caves beneath the sea. A cool breeze came from the ocean. Louise shuddered. "It's cold out here. And it's dark," she said. "Let's go inside."

Tom picked up one of the daggers. "Don't be afraid—if anyone tries to take our treasure, I'll defend it," he grinned.

"Don't joke," Louise begged. "It's scary enough out here. Do you suppose anyone was ever killed with that dagger?"

"If it was a pirate dagger, probably plenty of people were killed with it," Allen told her.

Louise shivered, and she insisted that they carry the treasure into the warm cottage. Allen stayed to turn out the light. Standing for a moment in the darkness, holding the smooth golden coin in his hand, he tried to imagine how the ship had been

wrecked. Had pirates stealthily climbed over her side on a dark, cool night like this one? Had they seized a sleepy sailor at watch on the deck and turned the quiet ship into a scene of raging, fighting men? Perhaps the pirates had taken most of her treasure, then scuttled her on purpose. Or perhaps the fight had led to flames that made the ship's gunpowder explode, scattering crew, pirates, and treasure, and even the ship itself on the bottom of the ocean.

Thinking of the pirates stealing up ladders on the dark side of the ship, Allen shuddered, too, as he turned toward the door. But out of the corner of his eye, he caught a shadow moving by the side of the house. Not daring to breathe, he looked again, standing motionless in the dark. Slowly, he made out the dark form of a man standing by the living-room window. He caught the outline of a man's figure. He had a beard! The man took a small shiny object from his pocket, looked at it, shrugged, and quietly walked away.

Allen slipped silently back into the house and told the others what he had seen. "I couldn't see his face. It was too dark," he said, "but I could see that he had a beard."

"There's nothing we can do," Tom finally said, "except make doubly sure he doesn't follow us to the treasure. And you keep a close lookout when you're in the boat alone, Louise."

Only a few days of vacation were left in which to work. They were busy hunting for the small pieces, busy taking them home and cleaning them. They did not decide what to do about the pieces they could not lift until the last day.

"We'll just have to wait until we come back next year," Tom said. "We have our maps and I've also marked the place on a larger chart of these waters. We'll divide up what treasure we have. When I get home, I'll do my best to see if any of the coins or other objects give me a clue to the ship. And, Allen, you see what you can find in the library in your city. There must be records somewhere in the world that will tell us about this ship."

"If you find out anything, write me," Allen said, "and I'll write you about anything I discover."

Tom and Louise saw the bearded man once again before their stay in Florida ended. They were carrying a bag of treasure along the shore when they came upon two men talking in low tones. Half-hidden, leaning against the side of a dock, the bearded man was deep in conversation with a grizzled old sailor. Before the bearded man could see them, Tom and Louise ducked behind a beach house and quietly made their way to Allen's cottage.

When Allen and his family left, two heavy boxes were added to the load their car carried from Florida.

STUDYING CHARACTER TRAITS

Listing Characteristics

As you read Chapter III silently, you listed the words which you thought described the characters. You probably listed kind, suspicious, and other traits.

Choose one student to be class secretary. Ask this student to make four columns on the chalkboard using the following headings:

| Tom | Allen | Louise | The Stranger |

Take turns dictating to your class secretary the character traits you have listed, and tell him the heading under which you wish each trait to be placed. Listen and watch carefully so that you will not repeat a characteristic which is already listed. When you have completed your class list, you may discover that you do not agree with some of the listings. If you do disagree, this will be a good time to discuss the reasons for the listings and to read orally the part or parts of the story proving your point of view.

Discussion of Character Traits

Sometimes several traits of character can be found in what a person or group of people decides to do. What character traits—

1. Made the three friends decide to let the nine-inch coral-encrusted ball drop back to the ocean floor?

2. Tempted Louise to talk to the stranger?

3. Convinced Allen and Tom that the stranger was not to be trusted?

4. Inspired the boys to plan to study the following winter about shipwrecks, coins, and other things related to their discovery?

5. Kept the three friends at their exhausting work?

CHAPTER IV

The Research That Paid Off

Tom and Allen spent most of the next winter studying and looking for information. They were doing research. Read the title of Chapter IV. What PURPOSE FOR READING does the title give you?

What clue to the outcome of the story does the title give you? When you use a clue in this way, you are making an INFERENCE.

The first letter Allen wrote to Tom was a warning written the day after he arrived home: "Be careful when you crack the coral on the treasures you haven't cleaned yet. I broke a glass bottle by accident today. I cracked the coral in the usual way, thinking I would find metal underneath, and broke the glass on the first hammer stroke. Anyway I still have the bottle, even if it is in three pieces now, and I may find another clue to the ship. I'm going to see if I can discover what country made glass like this and when it was made."

Whenever Allen went to the library that fall, he spent much of his time doing research on shipwrecks. He found several books written by divers about treasures on the bottom of the ocean. He learned about the tackle used to raise cannons and other heavy objects from the sea. He looked up *coins*, *glassware*, and *daggers* in the encyclopedia, and then read a book about coins. In it, he found a picture of a golden doubloon like the ones they had found.

"Have you come across anything that would tell us the name of the ship?" he asked in his next letter to Tom. "I've been looking for a list of Spanish ships that were lost or shipwrecked during that period, but haven't had any luck so far."

"I haven't done any research in the history of that period," Tom wrote back. "But I found out quite a lot about the time and money involved in raising a sunken ship. I'm convinced that we'll need lots of help to do it. In my reading, I've come across the names of people who have had experience with shipwrecks. If you agree, I'm going to write to these men."

Allen agreed to this plan and Tom acted at once. He wrote to six men. He kept the location of their shipwreck a secret, but asked them for information on raising sunken ships.

"I'm a little sorry you and I didn't talk to the bearded man," Tom wrote. "Since we've been home, Louise has told me more about him. He's an oceanographer, and he told her shipwrecks have been a hobby of his for a long time. He's been on many diving expeditions, and he is a diver himself. Since Louise doesn't remember his name, there's not much hope of ever finding him again. It's true there was a danger of his taking our treasure from us, but talking to him might have been worth the risk."

It was discouraging to learn they had been so close to an expert and now had lost track of him. Allen couldn't help but blame Tom for this. However, he forgave him after he received Tom's next letter: "I've received an answer to one of my letters, and luckily the man who wrote teaches in the university in your city. His name is Dr. Marco. Talk to him as soon as you can. You'll have to give him the general location of the shipwreck, of course, but he sounds like a good lead."

Allen telephoned Dr. Marco immediately and made an appointment for the next day. He found Dr. Marco in an office whose walls were covered with charts. Sea currents seemed to be Dr. Marco's special interest. When Dr. Marco shook hands with him, Allen saw the warmth and kindness of the lively brown eyes behind the doctor's glasses. He hardly noticed the short, well-trimmed beard.

Allen began by taking some of the coins from his pocket. All of them were cleaned now, and several gold doubloons gleamed in the pile he put on Dr. Marco's desk.

"Ah, yes," said Dr. Marco as he picked up a coin. "I've seen one like this within the last year. I spent my vacation at the Florida Keys last year. I go there every year. I talk to old sailors, and many of them spin yarns about treasure lying off the keys. Whether their stories are true or not, they tell some interesting tales. But last year, the most interesting thing I came across was an old coin a young lady showed me. It was like this one of yours."

Allen's mouth fell open. The young lady was Louise! Dr. Marco was the man with the gray beard! Poor Tom had spent months tracking down the very man he had been so anxious to avoid when they first found the ship!

Allen explained who he was. The doctor said that he had seen them carrying coral into Allen's cottage one evening last summer. He had come back later, but had looked at his watch, and decided it was too late to knock on the door. The shiny object Allen had seen in the hands of the

shadowy figure was only an old-fashioned pocket watch! Dr. Marco, the suspicious-looking, gray-bearded mystery-man, became Allen's good friend in the next few minutes. Allen saw why Louise had liked and trusted him.

They quickly got to work. "Here is a list of all the Spanish ships that are known to have gone down in the general area of the Straits of Florida," Dr. Marco said. "We can eliminate many of them, because their dates are too early to fit the dates on your coins. We shall have to examine your ship-wreck to learn her name, her cargo, and the size of her cannon. There will be records of all this in Spain. If any man survived, he would probably have made a report to the Spanish government. If we're lucky, his report may still be among government records in Spain. But, it may be that the ship was sunk by pirates and that no one lived to tell the tale.

"In any case, we may be able to interest a museum in raising the wreck during your next vacation. You have found a treasure. But I should warn you that unless there are many more doubloons, you probably won't get rich on it. Museums usually aren't rich; they depend on gifts for much of what they display. A museum would have to spend quite a lot of money to raise a cannon, clean coral and limestone from it, and stop the corroding action of the sea on the iron. Then they'd have to transport it. They might not be able to do much more for you than put a plaque bearing your name next to it."

"Do you think the Smithsonian Museum in Washington might be interested?" Allen asked. "I think Tom would be just as proud as I would be to have his name in the national museum."

"The Smithsonian is one of the museums I mean to contact," Dr. Marco answered. "If it's interested, you may be able to read your name there as the discoverer of a seventeenth-century Spanish ship."

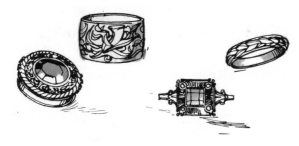

"Here's one thing I forgot to show you," Allen said, as he took a ring from his pocket. Inside the ring was an inscription almost worn away during the centuries the ring lay on the ocean's floor.

"I think you have a real clue there," the doctor said, his brown eyes shining with excitement as he studied the ring. "Just a moment—." He went to his bookcase and quickly leafed through a book.

After a moment, he nodded and closed the book. "This ring has a story to tell, and I think we can even guess that the ship you found was the Spanish galleon *Santa Anna*."

"How can you tell that by looking at the ring?" Allen asked in amazement.

"This ring was a present from the king of Spain to the governor of Panama," Dr. Marco explained. "That is the meaning of the inscription. In 1671 the country of Panama was invaded by a band of Englishmen led by a famous pirate, Henry Morgan. Although England and Spain were not at war at the time, the English and Spanish in the New World were never really at peace either. The English government didn't try to stop Morgan from looting the country of Panama. In fact, he was knighted in England three years later."

"But the ring?" Allen asked.

"The governor of Panama was killed by Morgan's men," the doctor went on. "This ring could have been part of the loot the pirates took."

"According to the rules of piracy, Henry Morgan should have divided the loot evenly among his

men. But, instead, he plotted to take it all for himself. One night after the pirates were asleep, his ship slipped away from the coast with most of the treasure on board. He took only a few members of his crew with him. The rest he left without ships or food.

"Morgan went to Jamaica and spent the rest of his life as a wealthy planter there."

"How does the ring fit in?" Allen asked again. "Morgan wasn't shipwrecked, and anyway he wouldn't have gone from Panama to Jamaica by way of the Florida Keys. They're too far north."

"You're right," said Dr. Marco, "I think your ship probably was the *Santa Anna*. We know that soon after Morgan's raid on Panama some English pirates seized the *Santa Anna* and killed most of her crew. The pirates put the rest of the crew in a small boat and sailed away in the *Santa Anna*. It was suspected that these pirates were the men that Morgan had deserted. The *Santa Anna* was never seen again. My guess is that it sank soon after—in 1671 or 1672. If I am right, we now know where she sank—on the reef you found off one of the keys. Some of the pirates were from Bermuda. If they were headed home, they would have sailed through the Straits of Florida."

"Whew!" said Allen. "Wait till I write Tom about this," he exclaimed. "We've been working on this for months and haven't found out the name of the ship. Yet you could tell me its name in a few minutes after you saw the ring."

Dr. Marco laughed. "You're wrong about the few minutes," he said. "It really took me much longer. I spent many years studying in order to know enough to unravel the story told by this ring."

"Will we ever know for sure if you're right?" Allen asked.

"Oh yes," Dr. Marco answered. "The number and size of cannon on the *Santa Anna* are known. We can also find out what cargo she was carrying when the pirates seized her." As he helped Allen gather up the coins, he said, "Write your friend, Tom, that when we meet again in the Florida Keys we'll try to have boats and tackle to bring up the remains of the ship you boys found."

Allen soon left, satisfied that the shipwreck now hidden on the ocean's floor would be raised. The treasures would be in museums where everyone could see the exhibits. And his name and Tom's would be on a plaque with the objects they had discovered. He hurried home, eager to write Tom the story of the *Santa Anna*. He whistled as he walked, jingling a pocketful of golden Spanish coins.

THINKING CAREFULLY

In this chapter Tom and Allen experienced different feelings at different times. Study this list. Some of them were experienced by the boys, and *some of them were not.*

Which ones did they feel? Read the part of the story to prove it.

inquiry	disinterest	regret
doubt	trust	shame
amazement	pride	security
satisfaction	hope	humor

Sometimes you read a good mystery story so rapidly that you miss clues which would have solved the mystery for you.

Did you miss clues which would have told you that—

1. The ship was really a Spanish ship of the seventeenth century?
2. The man with the gray beard was really not a suspicious character?
3. Tom and Allen could have trusted him?

Reread the story and discuss any clues you might have missed.

KNOWING WORD MEANINGS

1. Context Clues

Our word *context* comes from a Latin word which means "to weave or to knit together." The sentences we read in English are woven or knit together with words. Often when we meet a word we do not know, we can decide what it is because of the other words in the sentence. The other words give us clues to the meaning of the unknown word. When we get a meaning this way, we are using context clues to unlock the meaning of a word. What do the context clues tell us about the meaning of current in these sentences?

1. The strong current of water pulled the swimmer toward the reef.
2. The small plane was caught in a current of wind.
3. The flow of current causes the electric light to burn.
4. Current feeling places our team high in the standings.
5. The secretary reported on four current events from today's newspaper.

In each sentence above, current takes its meaning in part from the other words in the sentences.

Find each of the following words and tell what context clue helped you know the meaning of each word. Sometimes the context clue is in one sentence, but sometimes it becomes necessary to read several sentences or even several paragraphs before the meaning becomes clear.

Page 42, teredo   *Page 43*, sequence
Page 45, anticipate   *Page 41*, galleon

You will work with context clues many times in this reader.

If you did not know the meaning of each of the following words from a context clue, did you consult the Glossary or a dictionary?

Page 40, isolated   *Page 48*, gesturing
Page 56, accent   *Page 36*, coral

A very important reading skill for you to learn is to recognize when a context clue will give you the meaning of a word or when you must consult the Glossary or a dictionary for the meaning.

2. Structure Clues

a. Compound Words

Many words in English are formed by putting two words together. For example, in the story you have just read, something, forever, and forehead each contain two words used to form one. Such words are called compound words. When we form a compound word, each word which makes the compound often loses its meaning and the new word which it forms is given a new meaning, different from the meanings of the words which make it.

English is an important language with a large vocabulary. One reason for this is that English words often combine, or join, to create a new word with a new meaning. However, there are times when the words which make the compound keep their meanings. A good reader learns to recognize whether or not the meanings of the words which make the compound are changed in the new form.

On page 86 are clues to compound words used by the author of "The Mystery of the Gold Coins." After the clues, you will find a page number. See if you can make a compound word from the clues which are given you; then check the page and read the sentence in which the compound word is used. Give the meaning of the compound word and tell whether or not the meaning of the smaller words has been changed. The first one is worked out for you.

1. When you are beneath something, you are *under* it. You drink *water* every day. The compound word is <u>underwater</u> (Page 36). The compound word means under the water and does not change the meaning of the two smaller words.

2. A great star which is the source of the earth's heat is the _____. The opposite of dark is _____. The compound word is _____ (Page 37).

3. When you eat a bite of food, you open your _____. This apple has been divided. You may take the larger _____. The compound word is _____ (Page 37).

4. On a Christmas card you will often see an _____. Some people use worms to catch _____. The compound word is _____ (Page 45).

5. If you were a big game hunter, you would probably use a _____. If a lady had a shiny nose, she would use _____. The compound word is _____ (Page 65).

b. Words and Prefixes

Many English words change their meanings when we add a syllable called a PREFIX *before* them.

For example, when we add the prefix *un* to the word *lucky*, we make the different word <u>unlucky</u>. The meaning changes from lucky to "not lucky."

Here is a list of some words which were used in "The Mystery of the Gold Coins." Each of these words has a prefix. Tell how the prefix changes the meaning of the word to which it was added. If you need help, check the Glossary for meanings of the prefixes.

Page 36, **un**known   *Page 48,* **im**patiently

Page 42, **ir**regular   *Page 45,* **re**check

Page 47, **e**merged   *Page 41,* **a**ground

c. Words and Suffixes

Many English words change their meanings when we add a syllable called a SUFFIX *after* them. For example, *back* and the suffix *ward* will become <u>backward</u>, which means to move or to be directed back. Below is a list of words from your story. Each word has a suffix. Tell how the suffix changes the meaning of the word of which it is a part. If you need help to find the meaning of each suffix, see the Glossary.

Page 42, round**ish**   *Page 62,* suspic**ious**

Page 63, shadow**y**   *Page 73,* appoint**ment**

Page 64, dark**ness**   *Page 81,* pocket**ful**

Does the *ment* in equipment and in government mean the same in each word? Does the *y* in shadowy, discovery, and scary mean the same in each word?

3. Word History

Knowing the history of words often helps you understand new words. For example, the word biography comes into English from two Greek roots, *bio* meaning "life" and *graph* meaning "to write." A biography then is a writing about a person's life. *Auto* comes to us from the Greek; it means "self," so an autobiography is a person's own writing about himself. You read that Dr. Marco was an oceanographer. What is one thing an oceanographer does?

UNIT THREE
Reading Social Studies

PREVIEWING AND RECORDING

History is the story of great events in the lives of men. If you would understand the story of the past, study about the great men who lived in each age and find out what they did. Some great men have been explorers. Others have been rulers, inventors, scholars, missionaries, merchants, teachers, and so on.

Time and place are important in social studies. Events are important. Most important of all are the people you read about and the lasting effect their work has had on the world.

The accounts in your next unit will be about some famous explorers. There will be many details in the accounts. When there are many details you may become confused about which ones are important. Trying to remember them all is useless, if not impossible. For these reasons, an important part of becoming a better reader in social studies is to learn to RECOGNIZE IMPORTANT DETAILS.

After you have trained yourself to recognize the details which are important, you will have the problem of remembering them. Your PURPOSE FOR READING may be to find out *when* or *where*. You may need to know *who* or *what*. It will help you remember facts or KNOW WHAT YOU READ if you organize the details on a chart. Make a chart on a large piece of paper divided into three sections. (See illustration.)

Who	What and Where	When

Now turn to page 97. Hannu is the first explorer named. Place his name under *Who* at the top of your chart. *What* did he do and *Where* did he go? *When* did he go? Record this information on your chart. Be sure to record the question mark as you fill in the date. Scholars are doubtful about the accuracy of many early dates and use question marks to show this doubt.

Skim the rest of Chapter I and read the headings for Herodotus, Strabo, and Pliny the Elder. Record the information you get on your chart.

You now have some information before you start to read. This is one way of previewing a chapter. Previewing gives you an idea of what you are going to read about.

USING ILLUSTRATIONS TO PREVIEW

There are many ways to get information. Reading is one way, but don't forget to use other helps in your book. Many books have photographs, charts, graphs, maps, diagrams, and drawings in them. These illustrations are planned to give you a clearer understanding of the text you are reading. Turn to pages 90 and 91. What information do you get from these illustrations? Now skim the rest of Chapter I through page 109, and study the other illustrations. What different kinds of illustrations do you see? What information do you gain from them? Using illustrations is another way to preview.

UNDERSTANDING RELATIONSHIPS

You have previewed the headings and illustrations and have some background for the text you are going to read in Chapter I. You have learned *when* and *where*. They are important details. *Who* is another important detail. Any person who contributes important new knowledge to the world deserves to be remembered. *What* happened and *why* it happened are still more important details. If you know *what* and *why*, you can begin to see the relationship between the man's actions and ideas and the time in which he lived.

But most important of all is for you to understand the effect that the explorer's work has had on mankind. To do this, you must choose the important details and think carefully about the relationships between them.

CHAPTER I

Explorers from 2750? B.C. to A.D. 79

In Chapter I you will examine some ideas which were thought of more than 2,000 years ago. As you read the chapter through page 109, look for—
1. Ideas which seem strange to you.
2. Ideas which conflict with each other.
3. Ideas which are still true.

Man began exploring this planet long before he learned to write. No one is sure what part of the earth man first lived in, but most experts agree that man's first home was in Asia or Africa. Man's discovery of Europe was never recorded, nor do we know how or when the ancestors of the American Indians discovered America.

Historians have made many guesses about the discoveries which were made before man learned to write. But the only discoveries we can be sure of begin with written language. Many of the men you are going to read about in Unit Three left records of their work written in languages different from ours. These records have been translated (written in a different language) by scholars. Even after translation many of the words are difficult

and the sentences are long. For this reason the
translations have been rewritten but the meaning
has been kept the same. When you rewrite material
but keep the same meaning, you paraphrase.

The earliest exploration we know about was recorded in one of the world's oldest languages,
Egyptian.

Hannu

*Merchant who traveled to
the eastern coast of Africa
— in 2750? B.C.*

Writings on a temple in Egypt tell us the little
we know about Hannu, an explorer who sailed from
Egypt to the country we now call Somalia on Africa's eastern coast. Most historians say he made his
journey in about 2750 B.C. This early explorer is
so little known that you may not find him in your
encyclopedia. Do not mistake him for Hanno, who
lived many years later. The writings on the temple
have been translated to mean:

> I, Hannu, was sent to take ships to the
> land of Punt, to get spices for the Pharaoh.
> I arrived in port and had ships built to bring
> back products of all kinds. When I returned,
> my ship was full of products from Punt.
> I brought precious stones for the statues in
> the temple. There has never been a journey
> like this before.

Herodotus

Scholar who wrote history books and traveled in Greece, the Middle East, and North Africa — in 450? B.C.

Herodotus was a Greek scholar who spent seventeen years traveling. He visited Asia Minor, the islands of the Greek Archipelago, the western shore of the Black Sea as far north as the Dnieper River, and Egypt. In a book called *History*, Herodotus recorded most of what men in his day knew of history and geography. Some scholars have called him the "Father of History."

Herodotus tried to write the truth about the countries he saw himself, but he also wrote a great deal of hearsay in his book. Most of the stories he heard from others contained a great deal of untruth. Traders often made up stories about how and where they could find gold, spices, and incense. They wanted to keep the correct information a secret so that rival traders would not know where to go to trade for precious goods. Here is a brief selection from the *History:*

I must laugh when I see people drawing maps of the world without having much knowledge to guide them. Some make maps with an ocean stream running around the world, and others show the world as an exact circle, with Europe and Asia the same size. I will now tell the truth of this matter, making clear the size of each continent.

Europe stretches the entire length of Africa and Asia. It reaches far beyond Africa in the west. We know that Africa is surrounded by the sea, except where it is attached to Asia. An Egyptian king sent an explorer around its coast. He sailed south from eastern Egypt and sailed around as far as the Straits of Gibraltar, then came back to Egypt on the Mediterranean.

Of all the countries in the world, India lies the farthest east. It is from India that we get our gold. I have heard that this is the way they get gold in India: There are ants as large as dogs who live on the desert. Like the ants in Greece, this ant tunnels under the ground and makes mounds of sand around its hole. Many specks of gold are to be found in this sand and the Indians collect it. The giant ants chase the Indians when they see their golden sand has been stolen, but the Indians' camels are too fast for them. That is the way the Persians say the Indians get the gold.

Because Greece is in the center of the world, it has the best climate. On the other hand, the countries at the ends of the world produce the most excellent things. Besides the gold found in India, there are animals and birds much larger than anywhere else. There are also wild plants which bear wool, like sheep. The natives make their clothes of this plant-wool [cotton].

I have been in Egypt. I saw there the Nile River and the crocodiles for which it is famous. This is what crocodiles are like: In the winter for four months, they eat nothing. They have four feet and can live either on land or in water. Their eggs are laid on the shore. Of all known animals, this is the one that, from the smallest egg, grows to the largest animal. It has the eyes of a pig and no tongue.

Going west from Egypt, we find many different African tribes living on the shores of the Mediterranean. I cannot tell how far Europe stretches to the west, nor do I know of any Tin Islands [England] from which we get our tin. But it is certain that our tin and amber come from the ends of the world.

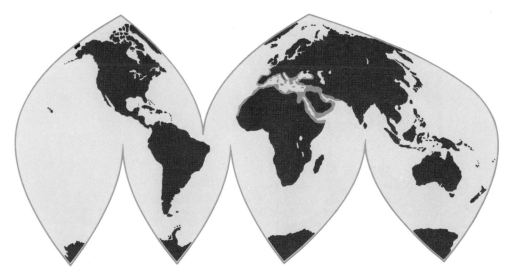

The known world in 450? B.C.

Strabo

*Geographer who traveled
about the Mediterranean Sea
and wrote a geography book
— in the first century A.D.*

Strabo was a Greek who wrote a seventeen-volume work on geography. He traveled widely although he did not visit all the countries he wrote about. As far as we know, Strabo's *Geography* is the first attempt to collect in one book all of man's knowledge of geography. His books are about Europe, Asia Minor, India, Egypt, and Africa.

By comparing his work with that of Herodotus, we can see how men's ideas about the earth changed from the fifth century B.C. to the first century A.D. Even before Strabo lived, a few mathematicians had been suggesting that the earth was a sphere. The following ideas are from Strabo's book:

> I assume in my book that the earth is a sphere. The roundness of the sea proves this. From the top of the ship's mast, a

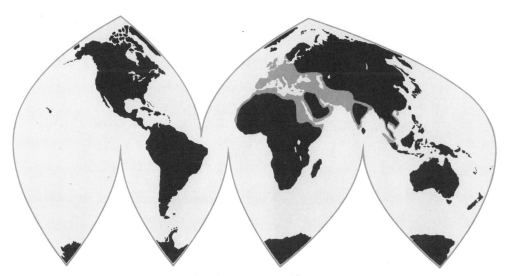

The known world in the First Century A.D.

sailor can see distant land that he cannot see when he is standing lower on deck. Sailors see shores rising as they sail toward the horizon.

The earth is an island on this sphere. We know this because whenever men have gone to the ends of the land they have met the sea. In the east the land of India is surrounded by water, and the land of Spain is surrounded by water in the west. As to the land we have not yet explored, there is very little of it. There may be some land east of India or west of Spain, but there cannot be much. Those who have tried to sail around the island of the world have not turned back because they met land, but because they were running out of food supplies.

Pliny the Elder

Historian who traveled in Europe and Africa and wrote natural history books — in the first century A.D.

Pliny the Elder, who was born in Italy, served in the Roman army and traveled with it to southern Germany. He also visited France, Spain, and Africa. He is famous for many volumes, all called *Natural History*. Pliny believed that Europe was the largest continent, Asia next in size, and Africa the smallest. Like Herodotus and Strabo, Pliny believed very far-fetched stories about people in the parts of the world he had heard about but had not seen. Here are a few of the ideas Pliny wrote in his book:

The Greeks were the first to divide the earth into zones. They noted what parts of the earth had days and nights of the same length during the same part of the year. They also noted the length of the

Parallel described
by Pliny the Elder

shadow made by a pole of a certain length
at noon during equinox. The equinox occurs
on the first day of spring and the first day
of autumn, when the day lasts exactly as
long as the night. The Greeks figured that
there were seven parallels which could be
drawn on maps and globes. [These parallels
were developed to help map the earth.]
Later three more parallels were added.

One parallel begins in that part of India
which faces south. It passes through Arabia,
Egypt, the part of Africa that is on the Mediterranean, the Strait of Gibraltar, and the
Atlantic Sea. At noon during the equinox, a
seven-foot pole standing on this parallel makes
a shadow no more than four feet long.
[Pliny then describes nine other parallels.]

Races of men are made in many different shapes and ways. In northern regions not far from where the north wind rises, there is a race of people with only one eye. It is in the middle of the forehead. This race carries on a continuous war with winged monsters for the gold that is in the mountains. Many authors, including Herodotus, have stated this.

In another country there is a race of people with their feet turned backward. They are extremely swift. These people cannot breathe in any air except the air in their own country, so none of them have been brought here.

CHECKING FACTS FOR ACCURACY

The men who wrote more than 2,000 years ago thought they were telling the truth except for the hearsay they wrote. If their facts were wrong, it was because they did not know the truth.

Make a list of the statements of fact as written by Hannu, Herodotus, Strabo, and Pliny the Elder that you now know to be false. Next make a list of their correct statements. Do you think that it is possible that some of the facts believed correct today may be proved to be incorrect in the future? Why?

MAKING A TIME LINE

The men you are studying in Unit Three lived at various times during the last 5,000 years. Dates are counted before and after the birth of Christ. Christ was born nearly 2,000 years ago. So something which happened 3,000 years before the birth of Christ would have happened nearly 5,000 years ago.

A time line is an important aid which will help you see and remember when important events happened. On a piece of paper make five lines, one for each 1,000 years. Divide each line into ten equal parts. Each part will stand for a century.

Since you have already read about four explorers in Chapter I, you can easily place their names on

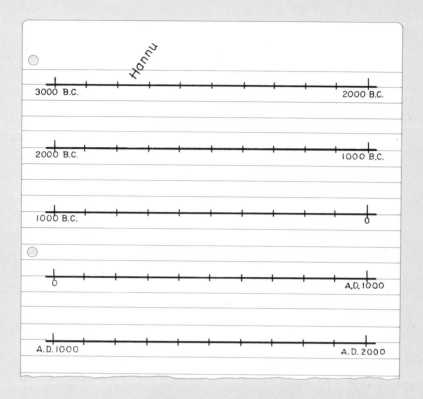

the time line. Hannu is placed for you. Where will you place Herodotus, Strabo, and Pliny the Elder? You will need to keep your time line for use as you study later explorers.

A time line makes a good class project, too. You can use a long space above your chalkboard. On a long piece of wrapping paper make a continuous line. Divide your line into five equal sections. Mark and label each thousand year period. Divide each period into ten centuries. Then locate each explorer on your time line as you read about him.

USING A MAP

Another way to help you remember details is to pinpoint on a map the different places that these explorers visited. This will need to be a class project. So you will need to make or secure a large outline map of the world. Place the map on a bulletin board so that you can pinpoint the places visited. Make small flags with paper and pins. Use a different color or design for each explorer. You may be able to find a picture of the flag or banner of many of the explorers. These would make interesting designs for your flags. Columbus, for example, sailed under the flag of Spain, but he also flew his own flag which you see pictured.

On each flag print the name of the explorer and the date of his exploration. Then pin the flag on the map to show where the explorer lived and traveled. Why will you need several flags for some of the explorers? Review Chapter I and pinpoint the four very early explorers with flags on your map.

Explorers from A.D. 1000 to 1522

Chapter II is about explorers who lived during a period of about 500 years. Their voyages and discoveries changed history and altered man's concepts of geography.

Preview the next chapter by filling in *Who*, *What* and *Where*, and *When* on your chart and discussing the illustrations.

Use the information from your chart and place each explorer's name on your time line. Why will all the names go on the first half of the fifth line?

After you have read about each explorer, pinpoint on your map the places he visited. You can plot their voyages by using colored string to join together the flags for each explorer.

The ideas of men are changing rapidly. Continue to watch for strange, conflicting, or false ideas as you read.

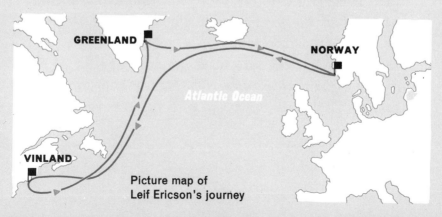

Picture map of
Leif Ericson's journey

Leif Ericson

*Discoverer of Vinland
— about A.D. 1000*

The discovery of the Americas was perhaps the most important of all recorded land discoveries. Eric the Red, a Norseman, had left Norway as a young man and founded a settlement in Greenland. Several years later his son, Leif Ericson, returned to Norway to visit his king. The king of Norway asked Leif to return to Greenland and spread the Christian faith. Leif agreed and set out upon his voyage to Greenland. He sailed west toward Greenland, but because of bad storms he went off course and came instead upon an unknown land. Many historians now believe that this land was the eastern coast of Canada or the northeastern United States. Leif Ericson was probably the first European to see America.

We know about Leif's adventure because it is told in the *Saga of Eric the Red.* This long story was spoken or sung in Iceland and Greenland for several hundred years before it was written. The *Saga of Eric the Red* was written sometime between 1305 and 1334. Neither Columbus nor any other southern European of his day knew about this *Saga*. The *Saga of Eric the Red* tells us:

After many stormy days Leif and his men saw land and sailed toward it. At high tide, their ship was able to enter a river and then beyond it a lake. There on the banks, they built themselves booths [huts]. There were many salmon both in the river and the lake, larger salmon than they had ever seen before.

They built a large house and Leif said to his men, "Let us divide ourselves into two groups so we can explore this country. Half of our party will remain in this house and the other half will explore the land. But they must walk away only until noon, so that they can come home each night. Thus we will not be separated." Leif himself went with the exploring party one day and stayed home the next. He was a large and powerful man, very wise and just.

One evening a man was missing. He was a good friend of Leif though he was not a Norse like the others, but a German. Leif set out with twelve men to find him. They

found the German at last, and he was in
very good spirits. "You have been lost,"
said Leif. "Why are you so happy?"

The German was so excited that he began
to speak in his own language and no one
could understand him. Finally he became
calm enough to explain in Norse, "I did
not go much farther than you, yet I have
found vines and grapes."

They slept that night in their booths
and in the morning Leif said to his shipmates, "Each day we will either gather grapes
or fell trees, until we have a cargo for our
ship."

Soon their ship was filled with dried grapes
and timber. When spring came, they made
their ship ready and sailed away to Greenland. Because of the vines in this land, Leif
called it Vinland.

Marco Polo

Traveler to China
who dictated a travel book
— in the late 1200's

Marco Polo was born in Venice, Italy. His father and uncle were merchants who traveled to other countries, buying and selling as they went. When Marco was seventeen years old, he set out with them to trade in the country of Cathay (China). The Polos were away from Venice for about twenty-four years. When they returned, Marco Polo was taken prisoner in a battle between the cities of Venice and Genoa and spent nearly a year in prison. While there he dictated the story of his travels to another prisoner. The prisoner wrote the story in French on parchment with a quill. It was later translated into seventy-five or eighty languages and each book was written by hand. It was not until 1477 that the book was first printed. Marco Polo gave a great travel book to the world.

Marco Polo's stories seemed to many people of his time less believable than the strange tales

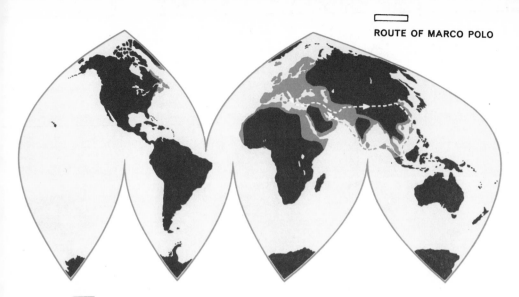

The known world in 1250

of Herodotus and Pliny the Elder. However, two of the most famous map and chart makers of the fourteenth century used Marco Polo's book as a guide for their maps and charts of Asia. They recognized his fine mind and his ability to observe carefully, and wanted to represent the known world using the facts Marco had reported. The book of Marco Polo begins:

> Great Princes, Emperors, and Kings! And people of all degrees who desire to get knowledge of the various races of mankind and of the cities of the world, take this book and cause it to be read to you. For ye shall find therein all kinds of wonderful things. [Marco Polo then described his route across Asia and told about the city Peking in China.]

The city where Kublai Khan had his court is square, six miles to each side. It has twelve gates, three on each side, and over each gate there is a great and handsome castle. The streets are so straight and wide that you can see from one side of the city to another, and great and beautiful houses are on the streets. All the plots of ground are square, so that the city is like a checkerboard, and it is so perfect that it is not possible to do its beauty justice.

Kublai Khan has a guard of twelve thousand horsemen. When he has dinner it is like this: In the great dining hall, his table is much higher than the others. At a lower level sit his sons and nephews, and at a lower level than that sit other noblemen. The wives of his sons sit lower still and at a level below them, the wives of other noblemen. The soldiers and officers sit on a carpet on the floor of the hall. The Khan can see them all, from one end of the hall to the other. Outside the hall are more than forty thousand people waiting to bring presents of gold and jewels to the Khan.

I will say nothing of the food they dine upon as you will imagine that there are many of every possible kind. When they have dined and the tables are removed, players come in and do wonderful tricks so that everyone is full of laughter. When the actors have finished, the company breaks up and each one goes to his own room.

On the Khan's birthday, the Khan wears a golden robe. Twelve thousand knights are dressed in robes like his, but less costly. Every man also has a golden belt, given to him as a present by the Khan. These suits have so many pearls and precious jewels that the cost of even one of them is beyond belief.

Christopher Columbus

Explorer who searched for
a western route to the Indies
and discovered
the New World — in 1492

The world owes a great debt to Columbus. He not only discovered the New World, which he never realized, but his successful voyages encouraged many other discoverers.

There are conflicting stories about the city of his birth and his life. However, we are certain that he was always interested in the sea.

At various times in his life he sailed on ships going to Greece, Spain, Portugal, and Africa. On these voyages he learned to use a compass and studied charts, maps, and globes. Finally he became such a good navigator that he was made captain on several voyages.

By this time Southern Europeans were demanding more and more of the precious products from the East. The journey over the Mediterranean, then across Asia and back again was long, dangerous, and costly. Traders and explorers were determined to find a cheaper, shorter, safer route.

Columbus, who believed that the earth was a sphere, was certain that this new route lay toward the west. He underestimated the size of the earth, however, and overestimated the size of Asia. He shared the belief of Toscanelli that Asia was only 3,000 miles west of Lisbon. Toscanelli, an Italian chart maker, was a student of astronomy, geography, and geology.

Columbus tried and failed to interest the king of Portugal in his planned voyage. He was success-

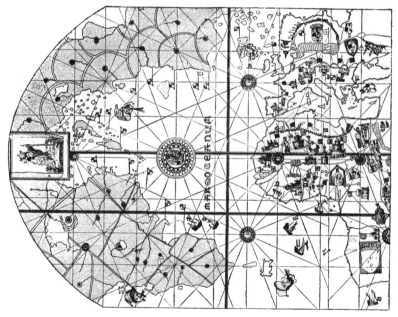

Chart drawn in 1500 by Juan de la Cosa, a pilot who had accompanied Columbus

ful in obtaining money for equipment and supplies from the king and queen of Spain.

Columbus owned a copy of the Latin translation of Marco Polo's book. On many pages of this book are notes in the admiral's own handwriting. This would lead us to believe that Marco Polo's book had much influence upon the discoverer of the New World.

The journal Columbus wrote on his first voyage to the New World has been lost, but a copy had been made. The man who made the copy sometimes copied word for word and sometimes changed the wording. In the paragraphs you are about to read, Columbus' own words are enclosed in quotation marks:

This is the first voyage and tells the way followed by Admiral Christopher Columbus when he discovered the Indies. On the first page he wrote this to the king and queen of Spain:

"Most exalted and most excellent and most mighty princes, king and queen of the Spains and of the islands of the sea: In this year of 1492 your Highnesses had heard of the lands of India and a prince who is called *Grand Khan* which means King of Kings. You sent me to see this prince and his peoples and lands. Your Highnesses ordered me not to go eastward by land, but to go by way of the west even though we did not know that anyone had ever gone that way before.

"Your Highnesses commanded that I should go to India with a fleet, and for this gave me the title Don, High Admiral of the Ocean Sea, and Governor of the islands and continents I should discover."

My ships sailed from the port of Palos on the third day of the month of August, 1492, on a Friday, half an hour before the rising of the sun. I steered my course for the Canary Islands, which are in the Ocean Sea [the Atlantic Ocean], and then set out on my way west to sail until I should reach the Indies and deliver your messages to the Khan.

"I thought to write carefully, from day to day, all that I might do and see. . . . To do this, I must forget sleep and these things will be a great labor."

October 10. The ships sailed west-southwest. They made ten miles an hour and, at times, twelve, and in the day and night together, they went 236 miles. The men could now bear no more; they complained of the long voyage. But the admiral held out to them bright hopes of the gains which

they could make. He added that they must go on until they reached the Indies.

Two hours after midnight [October 12] land appeared at a distance of about eight miles from them. Since the *Pinta* was swifter, and went ahead of the admiral's ship, it was a sailor on the *Pinta* who first saw land. They took in all sail, waiting for day.

In the morning they saw it was an island. They saw people at once and the admiral went ashore in an armed boat with the captain of the *Niña* and others. The admiral brought out the royal standard, and two other flags. When they had landed, the admiral called the two captains and the chief clerk who wrote the record of the voyage. Columbus said they should bear witness how he, before all, took possession of the island for the king and queen. Soon people of the island gathered there.

[In a later letter written by Columbus, he describes other islands he visited.] "These islands appear very fertile. Although it was November, the trees were blossoming and the birds were singing as they do in Spain in May. The people who live on the islands are very timid, and ran away from us until they saw that we would not harm them. I told the men not to give them things of no value, such as broken pieces of plates or old shoe straps. But if the natives did receive such things, they treated them like the most beautiful jewels in the world. It happened that a sailor traded a shoe strap for as much gold as would equal three golden coins.

"These people thought we came from heaven, and when we landed at a new village, the natives with us called, 'Come and see the people from heaven.' Then all the people visited us eagerly bringing food and drink."

Las Casas

Missionary to the New World
who wrote a history
— in the early 1500's

Las Casas was born in Spain. His father had traveled with Columbus on his first voyage to the New World. Las Casas graduated from a university in Spain and became a lawyer. He and his father accompanied Columbus on a later voyage to the New World and Las Casas stayed to help the Indians. He became the first priest to be ordained in the New World and was known as the "Protector of the Indians." Las Casas wrote a book called *The History of the Indies* which was not published until more than three hundred years later. In his book he expressed ideas like these:

It is clear that Admiral Don Christopher Columbus discovered our great continent. Amerigo Vespucci did great harm to the Admiral in giving himself credit for discovering the continent. Those who write of the continent now call it America as if it were first seen by Amerigo.

The Admiral Columbus left Spain on May 30, 1498, on his third voyage to the New World. He first saw the coast [of South America] in August of that year. Amerigo Vespucci was with another fleet that also landed on the mainland, but he was only a merchant and not the captain of a ship. Columbus had already reached the mainland before Vespucci's ships arrived there.

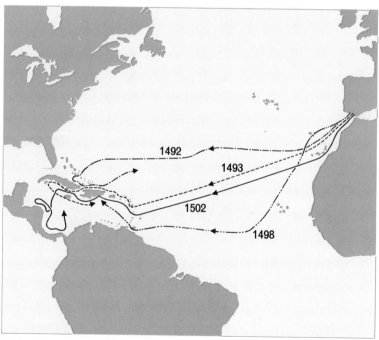

Columbus visits the New World

Vasco da Gama

Explorer who sailed around
Africa to India and then
returned to Portugal
—from 1497 to 1499

Vasco da Gama sailed from his country of Portugal to find an eastern sea route to India in 1497. He sailed around the continent of Africa and arrived in India in 1498. Columbus had opened the way to the western world, and now da Gama had found the sea route to the eastern world. There were several reasons why the sea route to the east had not been opened. First there was the superstition that men could not live in equatorial heat. Next, people believed that there were few inlets along the western coast of Africa. This meant that it would be difficult to get water or supplies and that there would be few safe harbors to seek during violent storms. Finally, the worst dangers they feared were the doldrums and the southeast trade winds. During the doldrums the ships might lie becalmed for long periods of time. If they were fortunate enough to outlast the doldrums, the southeast trade winds would blow directly against them.

Vasco da Gama discovered that the superstitions were false and overcame many other hardships. He completed the sea voyage to India. When he arrived in India he found that he was not welcome. Traders who had come by land from other countries did not want to lose their business and had influenced the Indians against da Gama.

Vasco da Gama was finally able to obtain samples of gold and spices which he took back to Portugal in 1499. The king of Portugal rewarded him and gave him the title "Admiral of the Sea of the Indies."

The following is from a book called the *History of India* written by an historian sixteen years after da Gama discovered his route to India:

To find out about the discovery of India, I asked older men who had sailed with da Gama about their voyage, and read the journals of some of the sailors.

For four months after leaving Lisbon, Vasco da Gama's three ships sailed south along the west coast of Africa. They landed on the coast from time to time to take fresh water and food on board.

When da Gama thought that they were near the Cape of Good Hope, he steered out to sea to avoid being driven on the shore by the stormy winds and then sailed southward. The winds were against them, so they traveled for a month without getting very far south. At the end of a month, they steered east, hoping to find that they had passed the Cape. But they saw land to the east.

"It may be that there is no end to the land," the pilots told da Gama. "We may find we cannot sail around it no matter how long we sail south."

Vasco da Gama assured them that the Cape was very near. He was not sure this was true, but he saw the men were afraid and might refuse to sail on. He told them to steer west again, then sail south.

It was winter in the southern hemisphere and the days were very short. The sea was covered with huge waves and in darkness much of the time. At night the lanterns on their masts were the only way the ships had of staying together. The wind was so strong that the crews were afraid the sails would be torn and the masts broken. With difficulty, the captains were able to make them sail south for two more months.

Finally da Gama ordered them to sail east. The seas were calmer there and they sailed for a long time without seeing land

to the east. Now they knew that they had rounded the Cape.

The good weather did not last long, however. As they sailed up the eastern coast of Africa, the winds became gales. The sea seemed to rise to the sky and fall back in heavy rains that flooded the ships. The men tied themselves to the masts so that they would not be swept overboard.

The storm continued for several days. The men of one ship were so frightened that they planned to capture their captain and put him in chains. Then they could return home. When da Gama heard rumors of this mutiny, he told his pilot to give him all the instruments he needed to chart the ship's course. Then he called his crew together on the deck, and called the crews of the other two ships to listen to his words.

Before them all, he threw the instruments into the sea. "You will never be able to return to Portugal without these instruments. From now on, I alone will chart the ship's course. Let no one speak to me of turning back, for if I do not find India, we will never return to Portugal."

Balboa

*Explorer who crossed Panama
and discovered
the Pacific Ocean — in 1513*

When Balboa, a Spaniard, was about twenty-six years old, he settled in Haiti and took up farming. He was unsuccessful and became greatly in debt. To escape his creditors, it is said, he hid in a cask marked "victuals for voyage" which was loaded on a ship headed for the Americas. The stowaway was discovered, but Balboa convinced the leaders of the expedition that he would be of more use to them as a soldier than as a prisoner. He later became governor of a Spanish colony which was in Panama. Balboa was bold, courteous, and kind. He soon gained the friendship of several native chiefs who told him of a great sea beyond the mountains. Balboa decided to secure the good will of the king of Spain by trying to discover this great sea. In September, 1513, he reached the Pacific Ocean and claimed all the lands it touched for the king of Spain. We do not have any account of this written by Balboa, but a Spaniard who heard of his deed wrote this to a friend:

We have messages from the New World. Balboa has attempted and accomplished a deed so great that not only has he been pardoned for treason, but given honorable titles.

The rumor had been heard by the colonists that beyond the high mountains to the west was an ocean rich in pearls. In between are lands rich in gold but the kings of the lands would defend them.

Balboa decided to try his fortune. He set out with 190 Spaniards and 1,000 natives on the first day of September in 1513 and began his journey. The journey covered forty-five miles and took twenty-four days. Partly by force, and partly by pacifying the native kings with presents, he scaled the mountains and saluted the ocean.

Balboa was the first European to see the Pacific from the shores of the New World. He was rewarded by the king of Spain, and was given the title "Admiral of the South Sea." He later had trouble with the jealous new governor of the colony on Panama. Balboa was falsely imprisoned for treason, was tried and sentenced to death.

Magellan

*Explorer who commanded the
first fleet to sail around
the world and discovered
the Strait of Magellan
— from 1519 to 1522*

Magellan was a Portuguese, but was serving a Spanish king on his most famous voyage. As you will see from this selection, however, Magellan did not live to complete the journey.

Magellan, like the other explorers, had to endure many hardships. In the first year of his journey one of his ships was destroyed by a storm, and another deserted and returned home. The captains and sailors he commanded were jealous and started a mutiny, which Magellan put down. Some of the men died from starvation on the ninety-eight day voyage across the Pacific. Their water supply ran low. They obtained food and water in the Philippines, but it was there that Magellan was killed.

The Spanish ships under a new leader sailed on without Magellan. Disaster struck two of the

ships, and in the end only one ship returned to Spain. The completion of this voyage was the first positive proof that the world was not flat.

Magellan left no record of his journey but one of his sailors kept a diary. The next section is from that diary:

Magellan had planned on a voyage over seas as yet unexplored; but he was careful not to tell too many people of it because the sailors might have refused to sail. On the 10th of August, 1519, we left Spain with five ships and sailed westward.

After nearing the coast of South America, we sailed south. We landed on the eastern coast to lay in a good supply of food. We traded with the natives and drove very good

bargains. They would give five or six fowls for a hook or a knife. A comb brought us two geese; a small mirror or a pair of scissors brought enough fish to serve ten people. For a little bell or a ribbon, they gave a basket of potatoes—the name they give to a food I have never seen before. Potatoes are roots a little like turnips in shape, and like chestnuts in taste. We also tried a kind of fruit [pineapple] that looks like the cone of a pine tree, but is very sweet.

Coasting southward along this land toward the Antarctic Pole, we stopped at two
islands where there lived geese [penguins]
and sea wolves [seals]. There were so many
geese, and they were so tame, that we caught
enough food for the crews of the five ships
in an hour. These geese are black and have
no wings with which to fly. They live entirely on fish.

The sea wolves are nearly as big as calves.
They have no legs and their paws are webbed

like a duck. We spent the winter [May to September in the southern hemisphere] on the eastern coast of South America. After much searching in the spring, we discovered and sailed through the Strait of Magellan.

On Wednesday, the 28th of November, we left the strait and entered the ocean which we afterward called the Pacific. We sailed for months without tasting fresh food. The biscuit we were eating was nothing but dust. We were so hungry we boiled leather and ate it. We even ate sawdust and rats.

Finally, in March, we found ourselves near an island [of the Philippines]. We landed here to find food and take care of the sick. Soon we began to have friendly meetings with the natives and began to thread our way through many islands. But we landed on one where the Indians were less friendly. Magellan became angry because the chief refused to say the king of Spain was the greatest king on earth. Magellan armed himself and his men, and went on shore to subdue this tribe.

To his dismay there were many Indians lined up on the shore when we arrived. Though our musket balls and arrows wounded them, we seldom killed them and they only attacked more angrily. When a poisoned arrow struck the leg of Magellan he ordered us to withdraw. Instead of withdrawing in an orderly way, most of the men turned and ran for the boats leaving the Captain, myself, and seven other men surrounded by Indians. The Indians, who outnumbered us so greatly, threw more spears at Magellan than any of the rest of us. Finally, he fell. Thus perished Magellan, our guide and our light.

On the 8th of September, 1522, we re-entered our home port in Spain. Of five ships and about 240 men who left Spain in 1519, one ship and 18 men returned. All the others deserted, died of sickness or starvation, or were killed.

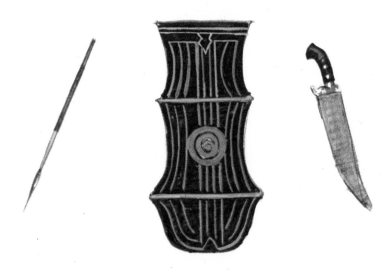

THINKING ABOUT GOALS

If you have completed your chart and brought your time line up to date, you have a record of *Who*, *What* and *Where*, and *When* of the explorers through 1522. But how were they able to do these things, and why did they do them?

Why does an explorer start on a long journey into unknown regions, over waters where man has never sailed before, over lands covered with swamps, and forests where there is no road? What is the goal? What is the reward? Were these explorers seeking wealth, a better way of life, adventure, new empires, knowledge, or the spread of the Christian faith? Not all of them were looking for the same things.

The explorers who traveled between the time of Leif Ericson and Magellan discovered many parts of the world heretofore unknown to Europeans. Their new knowledge of the world, which they reported, was as exciting to people then as space flights are to us today.

When we read about the explorers we must remember that most of them were sent on their journeys by rulers of countries. These rulers wanted to build empires as well as find riches. The European countries bordering on the Atlantic Ocean were especially active in empire building. Portugal and Spain were the first. Holland, England, and

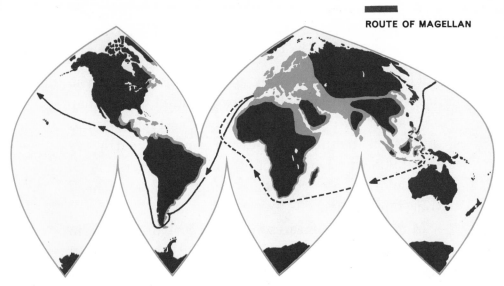

The known world in 1522

France soon rivaled them. All wanted to claim riches and new lands.

The work of all the explorers together changed man's view of the world. By 1522, the major regions of the world, with the exception of the Poles and Australia, had been discovered. This does not mean that the interior of the continents had been explored fully, or that the world was accurately mapped. It does mean, however, that man had broken through centuries of fear, ignorance, and superstition. The groundwork was being laid for a scientific study of the earth and its people—a study which continues in our time.

RECOGNIZING WHEN YOU NEED
MORE INFORMATION

The routes traveled by the seven explorers you have studied in Unit Three are pictured on the map on page 143. Notice that only the known world of 1522 is pictured. What parts of the earth are still unknown? Do the routes of the explorers match your plotting on your class map? If not, recheck your information.

Many other venturesome and curious men who were exploring at this same time and later are listed on the chart which follows.

These men were chosen because of their interest in the Americas. Included in the list are explorers through the year 1730. If you would have

---

EARLY EXPLORERS
OF THE WESTERN HEMISPHERE

JOHN CABOT — England
JUAN PONCE DE LEON — Spain
HERNANDO CORTES — Spain
FRANCISCO PIZARRO — Spain
JACQUES CARTIER — France
MARTIN FROBISHER — England
SAMUEL DE CHAMPLAIN — France
JOHN SMITH — England
RENE ROBERT DE LA SALLE — France
VITUS BERING — Russia

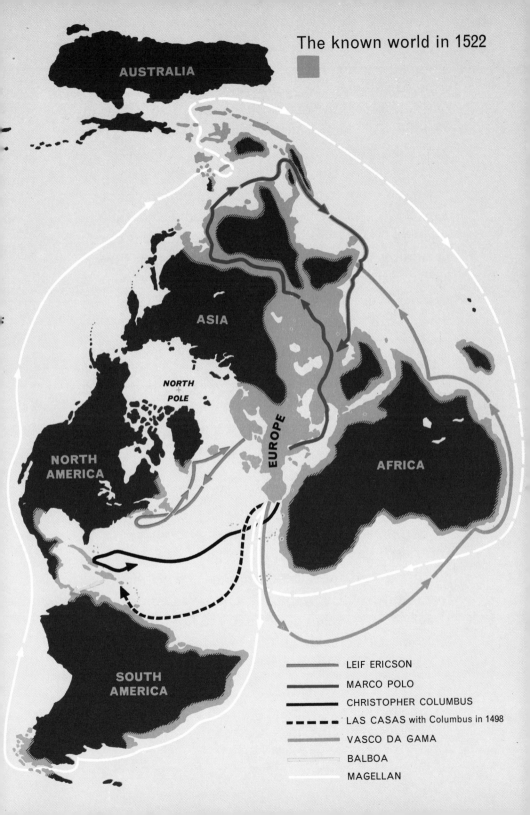

The known world in 1522

AUSTRALIA

ASIA

NORTH
POLE

NORTH
AMERICA

EUROPE

AFRICA

SOUTH
AMERICA

LEIF ERICSON
MARCO POLO
CHRISTOPHER COLUMBUS
LAS CASAS with Columbus in 1498
VASCO DA GAMA
BALBOA
MAGELLAN

a more complete understanding of this period, you will want to read about some of these other explorers. You have learned how to LOCATE INFORMATION OUTSIDE YOUR TEXT. You know the value of using the index and the table of contents when you need to locate information in a book. You have been using the encyclopedia and the dictionary. Maps and illustrations have been helpful in adding to your store of knowledge. The library card catalogue in your school or public library is another valuable aid. Most library card catalogues have cards arranged alphabetically according to subject, title of book, and author. Learn to use these cards and you will be able to locate sources of information very quickly. Study the three sample cards which are illustrated. What information do you gain from each card? Why is it helpful to have three different cards which give the same information?

Not only do you need to know how to locate additional information, but it is also very important for you to RECOGNIZE WHEN YOU NEED MORE INFORMATION. Do you know enough about the explorers listed on page 142 to report on them and to fill in your chart, time line, and map? If not, you can readily see that you need more information to complete your knowledge of this period in history. Use other sources to gain the information you need.

XBC
327A **Averill, Esther Holden.**
Cartier Sails the St. Lawrence, retold by
Esther Averill; illus. by Feodor Rojankovsky.
Harper & Row, 1956.

> 108 p. illus. maps
> A retelling of the exciting true story of Jacques Cartier's
> three expeditions to the New World in search of the Northwest
> Passage, and of his discovery of the St. Lawrence River.
> Information taken largely from Cartier's own log books.

> 1. Cartier, Jacques, 1491–1557.

XBC Cartier Sails the St. Lawrence.
327A **Averill, Esther Holden.**
Cartier Sails the St. Lawrence, retold by
Esther Averill; illus. by Feodor Rojankovsky.
Harper & Row, 1956.

> 108 p. illus. maps
> A retelling of the exciting true story of Jacques Cartier's
> three expeditions to the New World in search of the Northwest
> Passage, and of his discovery of the St. Lawrence River.
> Information taken largely from Cartier's own log books.

> 1. Cartier, Jacques, 1491–1557.

XBC CARTIER, JACQUES, 1491-1557.
327A **Averill, Esther Holden.**
Cartier Sails the St. Lawrence, retold by
Esther Averill; illus. by Feodor Rojankovsky.
Harper & Row, 1956.

> 108 p. illus. maps
> A retelling of the exciting true story of Jacques Cartier's
> three expeditions to the New World in search of the Northwest
> Passage, and of his discovery of the St. Lawrence River.
> Information taken largely from Cartier's own log books.

> 1. Cartier, Jacques, 1491–1557.

REVIEWING BETTER READING RULES

To UNDERSTAND RELATIONSHIPS in social studies, all of the reading rules listed on page 13 need to be used. Study this "tree" of understanding relationships and discuss how each branch is an important part of this skill. The wording of the branches has been shortened. See if you can match each branch with the complete rule on page 13. Which branch cannot be matched? Of which rule is it a part?

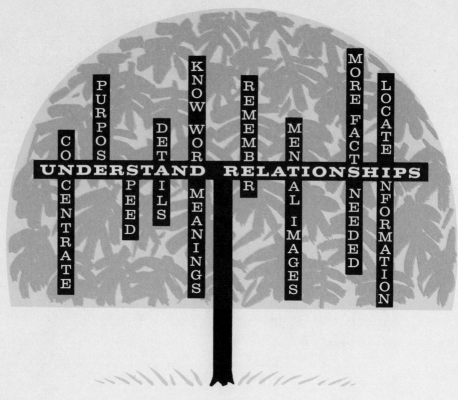

To UNDERSTAND RELATIONSHIPS, you need to know facts. Can you answer these fact questions?

1. How much land was Balboa claiming for the king of Spain?

2. What important statement did Las Casas make in his writings?

3. Why did Columbus make his first voyage?

4. Was Leif Ericson's discovery a planned or accidental one?

5. What uses were made of Marco Polo's book?

Now make up some fact questions on Chapter II to ask your classmates. Study the text carefully so that you are sure the questions can be answered. Be sure you are asking a question which involves an important detail.

One of the following questions involves an important detail and one an unimportant detail. Can you tell the difference?

1. How many fowls did Magellan's men trade for a hook or a knife?

2. What kinds of foods were Magellan's men able to bargain for?

Can you answer these relationship questions?

1. Why didn't Columbus know of Leif Ericson's discovery?

2. How did the stories of Marco Polo influence explorers who followed him?

3. Why was da Gama so determined to reach India?

4. Why did Marco Polo say, "Take this book and cause it to be read to you"?

5. The great countries in North and South America are described as Christian nations. The main languages spoken in these countries are English, French, Portuguese, and Spanish. What is the relationship between these two statements and the information given on pages 140 and 141?

Now, compose other relationship questions to ask your classmates. Be sure that there is enough information in the text or from your reports for your classmates to draw conclusions. Remember, relationship questions are harder to write, and the answers require more thinking than do fact questions.

Composing good questions based on the selections you have read is an excellent way to review.

Animals seen in new lands

CHAPTER III

Explorers from 1768 to 1873

Preview Chapter III on explorers from 1768 to 1873. Fill in your chart and study the illustrations. As you read about each explorer, add his name to your time line and pinpoint his explorations on your map. Continue to check on accurate, false, and strange ideas of the explorers.

James Cook

*Explorer of the eastern
coast of Australia,
who voyaged around the world
—from 1768 to 1771*

Beginning with the last half of the sixteenth century fewer expeditions were made by men from countries in southern Europe, and more were made by people from northern Europe. To continue the unrolling of the map, the thoughts of many explorers turned toward Australia. French, Portuguese, Dutch, and Spanish explorers all claimed knowledge of Australia. Much of this knowledge was kept secret because of fear of competition. Scholars believe that the Dutch were probably the first to go ashore on the north coast of Australia and were the first to discover its west coast.

An Englishman, James Cook, voyaged around the world in the years from 1768 to 1771. He was able to take advantage of all that man had learned about navigation and exploration since Magellan's men had made the first voyage around the world in 1519–1522. Cook was one of the first explorers to record discoveries with scientific accuracy. A naturalist and an astronomer sailed with him and kept their own records. Cook was the first man to cross the Antarctic Circle. He believed that there was land (Antarctica) within the circle but he never saw it.

Cook sailed westward across the Atlantic from England. He rounded South America, crossed the Pacific, and spent some time in New Zealand. These selections are taken from the journal Captain Cook kept on his first voyage around the world:

Saturday, March 31, 1770. I was ready to leave New Zealand and began to plan the best way to return to England. I wished to return by Cape Horn because I wanted to discover if there was a continent lying between New Zealand and South America. Since winter was coming on in the southern hemisphere, I decided against this. For the same reason I decided not to go to the Cape of Good Hope. Therefore I planned to sail westward to the East Indies and to explore the ocean to the north.

Thursday, April 19, 1770. Gales and cloudy weather with a large sea. We saw land [Australia].

Friday, April 20, 1770. The weather was clear. The country was pleasing with hills, ridges, plains, and valleys. Most of it was covered with trees.

Saturday, April 21, 1770. In the P.M. we saw the smoke of fires in several places, a certain sign that the country is inhabited.

Saturday, April 28, 1770. We saw several people ashore. A few of us left the ship and rowed toward the shore but we could not land because the surf was too rough. The natives hid as we approached which disappointed us. We did see small canoes like those in New Zealand and palm-like trees. This was all we were able to see and so we returned to the ship. Later we discovered a bay [five miles south of the present site of Sidney].

Sunday, April 29, 1770. We anchored in the bay and approached the shore in small boats. There were people on the shore but they all ran away except two men who seemed determined to prevent our landing. I threw some beads and nails ashore. The men picked them up and waved their arms. I thought that they wanted us to land, but when we tried, they threw darts at us. I fired my musket several times; the men ran away and we landed. We looked for fresh water and finally found a small stream. This stream and fresh water from holes dug in the sand gave us a chance to fill our casks.

Monday, April 30, 1770. While we were getting wood and water, sixteen natives came to within 100 yards of us. We offered them presents but they refused them. They were armed with darts and wooden swords. The darts have four prongs and are pointed with fishbones. They seem to be for fishing rather than war and are not poisoned as we had thought.

Sunday, May 6, 1770. I decided to call this bay Stingray Bay. [Later the name was changed to Botany Bay because of the great number of different plants on its shore.] During our stay I have caused the English colors to be flown every day. Since we have been unable to convince the natives that we are friendly, I decided to leave this bay and continue northward along the coast.

Cook sailed northward along Australia's eastern coast. He needed all of his ability as a navigator to steer the ship through dangerous waters. Again and again the ship was in peril and the dangers increased until the vessel finally went aground. A dangerous leak resulted. Cook finally found a harbor which he entered after several days' delay because of the weather.

Saturday, June 23, and Sunday, June 24, 1770. While in the harbor to repair the ship

we have sent parties ashore to explore the
land. One of the men saw an animal [kan-
garoo]. It was of a mouse-color, very slender,
and swift of foot. Its tail was very long, and
its manner of running reminded me of a
rabbit or deer.

Tuesday, July 10, 1770. Four natives were
on the shore. We paid no attention since
we did not want to frighten them. Finally

two of them came in a canoe and we tossed beads to them. They returned to shore and brought the other two to our ship to take more presents. When they returned to the shore we followed them and stayed with them until dinnertime.

Wednesday, July 11, 1770. Gentle breezes from the land and sea. We aired the bread, stowed away water, and did other necessary work. Some of our men caught a large turtle and some shellfish. Four natives paid us a visit. They seem to be more friendly.

Thursday, July 19, 1770. We are getting ready for sea. Ten or eleven natives visited us. They grew a little troublesome and started throwing things overboard. I offered them bread which they rejected. Soon afterward they went ashore. Several of our men went ashore and immediately upon their landing one of the natives took a handful of dry grass and lighted it at a fire. Before we knew what was going on he made a large circle around us and set fire to the dry grass. Some of our young pigs were scorched to death, but we got the fire out before it got its head.

Saturday, August 4, 1770. We set sail today as a longer delay would use up our supplies of food. We have yet a long passage to make to the East Indies through unknown and dangerous sea.

For many weeks Cook sailed among dangerous reefs. At one time he nearly lost his ship. Finally he reached the open sea to the west and returned to England by way of the Cape of Good Hope on June 12, 1771. He could claim only the coast of Australia for England, because of the hostility of the natives.

Lewis and Clark

Explorers of
Louisiana Territory
—from 1804 to 1806

Lewis and Clark made a major journey of discovery for the United States Government. Both men knew how to live in wild country and both knew some of the languages spoken by the Indians. Their exploration of the Louisiana Territory started by canoe near St. Louis on May 14, 1804.

On their expedition Lewis and Clark surveyed the land to find the best route to the Pacific. They made careful records of everything they learned about geography, Indian language and customs, and plant and animal life. They did their best to make friends with the Indians they met.

At the time of the following selection the expedition had divided into two groups. Lewis and three men were traveling overland hoping to buy horses from the Indians. Clark and the main party were bringing the expedition's equipment by canoe. They

157

planned to meet near what is now the border of southwestern Montana:

August 13, 1805. We [Lewis and three companions] met an Indian tribe. We smoked a pipe of peace. When the chief learned that we had tasted no food that day he gave us cakes made of dried berries. Later the chief invited Captain Lewis to taste a bit of boiled antelope meat and some roasted fresh salmon. This was the first salmon Lewis had seen. He was now sure that we were nearing the Pacific. We stayed the night in the Indian's camp.

August 14, 1805. Captain Lewis decided to spend the day near the Indian camp, because in two days he was to meet Captain Clark at a fork between two rivers only a few miles west. Having nothing to eat but flour, dried meal, and the Indians' berries, Lewis, his men, and Indians went out to hunt.

Although the Indians killed no game on this day, we were able to see how they hunt. About twenty Indians armed with bows and arrows went out riding on fine horses. When they saw a herd of antelope, they separated into groups of two or three and circled the animals. The circle was about five miles around, and the warriors did not come near the antelope until the circle was formed.

Then one small party rode toward the herd. The horses were skilled at keeping their footing in this broken country, running at full speed down steep ravines and along the edges of cliffs.

The antelope ran swiftly, but met a fresh party coming from the opposite side of the big circle. The antelope turned in another direction, but here too they met new enemies. The Indians hoped to chase them back and forth until they became so tired that they could hit them with arrows.

All the antelope escaped today, though the chase was beautiful to watch. On this day, our own men could not kill any game either, so we ate only a paste made of flour, water, and berries.

Captain Lewis asked the chief to give him men and horses. He promised to pay them well when we met Captain Clark. The chief agreed, but many of the warriors feared we would lead them into a trap laid by their enemies. Only six or eight warriors said they would come with us.

August 15, 1805. About noon we left camp on foot. The Indian chief and his warriors were on horseback. At sunset we made camp. One of our men had been sent forward to hunt, but he returned in the evening without game. Our only supper was flour stirred in boiling water. We divided it among the four men in our party and two of the Indians.

August 16, 1805. As neither our party nor the Indians had anything to eat this morning, Captain Lewis sent two hunters ahead. This made the Indians more suspicious than ever of being led into a trap. Some of them rode ahead on their horses to watch the movements of our two men.

Just as Captain Lewis and one man started on their day's march, one of the Indian scouts came dashing over the plain. He said one hunter had killed a deer. Captain Lewis shared the deer with the starving Indians. Later two more deer were brought in, which he also shared.

In the afternoon, we reached the fork of the two rivers where we were to meet Captain Clark. Captain Lewis was dismayed to find he was not there. If the Indians refused to stay, we would lose our chance to buy horses for the overland trip ahead. By promising them presents, Captain Lewis managed to persuade most of them to stay over night.

August 17, 1805. Early in the morning an Indian scout told Lewis he had sighted white men in canoes on the river. The Indians were as happy as we were with the news, for they now saw that we had told them the truth.

The canoes soon came into camp, and the parties were together again, to the relief of both Captain Lewis and Captain Clark. After Captain Clark's party had carried the equipment from the canoes, we gave medals, clothing, tobacco, and knives to the Indians. They promised to return to their village and bring us horses on which we could load the equipment which had been carried by canoe.

The expedition pushed on and reached the mouth of the Columbia River on November 15. They had traveled four thousand miles and had seen many heretofore unknown Indian tribes. They had made valuable scientific collections and were the first explorers to cross the continent within the limits of the United States. The next spring the expedition returned to St. Louis. Hardship, peril, and exposure had been overcome by all but two of the original expedition. One member had deserted and one had died.

David Livingstone

Missionary who
explored Africa
— from 1840 to 1873

Henry M. Stanley

Newspaperman sent to Africa
to look for Livingstone
— in 1871

David Livingstone was a Scottish missionary who belonged to the London Missionary Society. He did more than any explorer of his time to make known to Europeans the interior of Africa. In many years of exploration he traveled from the cape to the equator and from the Atlantic to the Indian

163

Ocean. In 1871 he was trying to find the source of the Nile River. He had been exploring Africa for so long that people had almost forgotten him or believed he was dead.

The *New York Herald* sent Henry M. Stanley, a reporter, to find Livingstone. Stanley began his African trip at Zanzibar. He carried cloth and beads to trade for food with the natives. This selection is taken from the account of his journey which he wrote for the newspaper:

October 1, 1871. We camped under a tree so large that all of my party was beneath its boughs. I thought of the man I had come so far to find. Though I had never seen him, we were on the same soil, perhaps in the same forest. I kept asking myself, "Is he still alive?"

October 2, 1871. We crossed a plain today. The sun was very hot, but there were enough trees to cast shade. Only the swarms of flies made our march difficult.

After a few hours, we saw two giraffes. We had now entered game country, and our supply of food was low. However, we found no game before we camped.

The men went to sleep tonight hungry, cross, and ready to desert me. If they leave me, I will have to give up my search for Livingstone.

November 3, 1871. This morning we met

a tribe of 80 men. They told us that an old man had just arrived on the southwestern shore of Lake Tanganyika. The more I questioned them, the more I knew that the man must be Livingstone.

November 4, 1871. Started early. Guides were sent forward so we might be warned if they saw war parties. We were completely silent. The first part of the march was through a jungle of small trees. The jungle became thinner and thinner until we entered a treeless plain.

On the plain we came across villages. Many of the chiefs asked for cloth or beads in payment for letting us pass through their country. I soon saw that if we paid to pass through every village we would not have enough cloth to pay for our journey back to the coast. We were too near Livingstone to give up; I could not fail for lack of cloth. I decided we would try to sneak past the villages at night.

November 8, 1871. Today we came to a forest and were soon deep within it. No road was near. We kept deep silence. A few more hours would see the end of my long search. Patience!

November 9, 1871. Last night we slipped silently by one more village. At last we are past the tribes that would have taken our cloth. Tonight I had a new suit laid out. The clothes I have worn in the jungle are rags, and tomorrow I hope to see Livingstone.

November 10, 1871. It is a happy morning. The air is fresh and cool. After two hours of walking, we came to the top of a hill and saw below a beautiful broad sheet of water— Lake Tanganyika!

At this moment, we do not think of the hundreds of miles we have marched or the hundreds of hills we have gone up and down. We forget the many forests we have crossed, and the hot suns that have scorched us. At last our dream is coming true. We are near the village in which we hope soon to find Livingstone.

We met natives outside the village who told us that Livingstone is indeed here. One of them ran to tell Livingstone that we have come. The native returned, saying the doctor was so surprised he didn't believe him. By the time we reached the center of the village, however, he was waiting in front of his hut with a group of natives. When I saw the white-haired man, I felt shy. Instead of throwing my arms around him as I wished, I greeted him as coolly as if we were on a street in London. I took off my hat and held out my hand saying, "Dr. Livingstone, I presume."

Stanley and Livingstone explored the area around Lake Tanganyika. Near the end of the year the two explorers started eastward. Stanley tried to persuade Livingstone to return to England where praise and comfort waited for him. Livingstone refused because he felt his work in Africa was not finished. On March 15, 1872, Stanley gave Livingstone some supplies and bade him farewell.

QUALIFYING STATEMENTS

When writers do not have complete information or when they are doubtful if the facts they state can be proved, they often qualify their statements. They use words such as: *usually*, *perhaps*, *some people believe*, and many others to show that they question the accuracy of the statements they are reporting. On page 111 you read, "Leif Ericson was *probably* the first European to see America." What qualifying word was used? Why could the accuracy of this statement be questioned?

What qualifying words are used in these sentences from Unit Three?

1. No one is sure what part of the earth man first lived in but most experts agree that man's first home was in Asia or Africa.

2. This would lead us to believe that Marco Polo's book had much influence upon the discoverer of the New World.

3. To escape his [Balboa's] creditors, it is said, he hid in a cask marked "victuals for voyage," which was loaded on a ship headed for the Americas.

Find more examples of qualification of statements in Unit Three of this text and in any other reading you do. Discuss with your classmates the reason for such qualifications.

One of the ways to become a better reader and to have more accurate knowledge is to watch for qualified statements.

In your own reports, both written and oral, be sure you qualify your statements when you are not certain of their accuracy.

STUDYING CHARACTER TRAITS
AND
MAKING INFERENCES

A good way to help you understand people or characters in books is to look for traits of character. Sometimes in books these traits are very evident because of such statements as, "Balboa was bold, courteous, and kind." Sometimes you need to read carefully and make an inference to discover a character trait. What do you infer from this: "Balboa convinced the leaders of the expedition that he would be of more use to them as a soldier than as a prisoner"?

Find examples in Unit Three of character traits which are mentioned and those traits which are inferred. Discuss the inferences you make with your classmates.

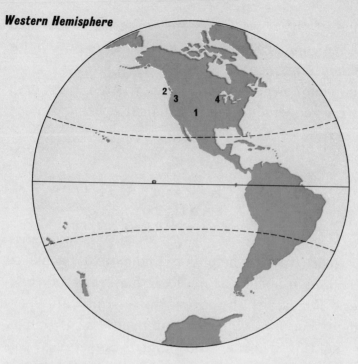

Western Hemisphere

1. ZEBULON PIKE

2. GEORGE VANCOUVER

3. ROBERT GRAY

4. LOUIS HENNEPIN

RECOGNIZING WHEN YOU NEED MORE INFORMATION, AND DOING RESEARCH

When you finished reading and discussing Chapter II, and reported on other explorers from the years 1000 through 1730, you had a more complete picture of the explorations of that period in history.

More information about the explorers of this period (1768–1900) will be necessary to complete

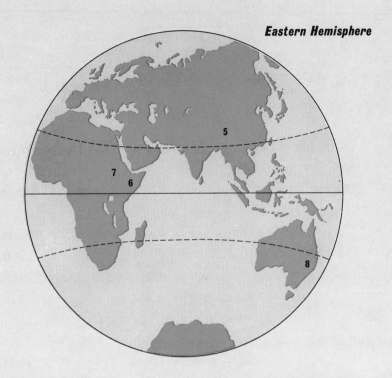

Eastern Hemisphere

5. SVEN HEDIN   7. JAMES BRUCE

6. SIR RICHARD FRANCIS BURTON   8. WILLIAM WENTWORTH

your knowledge of this time in history. On each hemisphere are small figures indicating a new exploration area. Use the figure and the legend of the map to discover the area each man explored. Prepare reports on these men. Be sure your report is interesting, and be sure also that the facts you give are important and accurate. If you are uncertain of the accuracy of your information, be sure to qualify your statements.

CHAPTER IV

The Twentieth Century

Man has always been curious about his environment. As soon as he learns what is near by, he becomes curious about what is just beyond. He is still exploring new places.

Chapter IV tells about five explorers who have lived in the twentieth century, that is, since 1900. They have gone to the polar region, into outer space, and below the surface of the sea. Each one is important because he was the first to explore a new region.

Before you read, preview the chapter. Add each explorer to your chart telling *Who*, *What* and *Where*, and *When*. As you read about each explorer, add his name to your time line and pinpoint his exploration on your map. How are you going to pinpoint the space and underwater explorers?

By 1900 man had mapped most of the earth's surface. Only the polar regions remained almost completely unexplored, and it is therefore in the arctic and antarctic that the early twentieth-century explorers have done much of their work. Both the North Pole and the South Pole were discovered in our own century.

Robert E. Peary

*Discoverer of the North Pole
— in 1909*

Several attempts had been made to reach the North Pole before Robert E. Peary reached it in 1909. Using dog sleds, he started from Cape Columbia on Ellesmere Island on March 1. Part of his party turned back, but Peary, four Eskimos, and another American started north with five sledges pulled by 40 dogs. Although the North Pole is in the Arctic Sea, it was possible for Peary to walk to the Pole because the sea is covered with ice. The ice often cracks and moves. Peary and his men sometimes traveled north while the ice they were on moved south. For this reason they traveled much farther than the actual distance from Ellesmere Island to the North Pole. This is from Peary's book, *The North Pole:*

The second day of April was a fine marching morning, clear and sunlit. The temperature was minus 25 degrees. The ice floes were large and level except for the pressure ridges. The ice fields to the north, the brilliant blue sky, the biting wind, all reminded me of Greenland.

We had to hurry to get to the pole before the full moon stirred the tides and caused the ice to crack. [Ocean tides are highest when there is a new moon or a full moon. The movement of the water caused by the pull of the full moon makes the polar ice crack more often than at other times of the month.]

At the end of a ten-hour march, I came to a lead which was just opening. It was ten yards wide in front of me, but a few hundred yards to the east I saw a place we could cross. I signaled to the men with the sledges to hurry. We got the sledges over cracks so wide that the men had difficulty jumping them.

While we were building igloos for our camp, we could see a wide lead opening east of us. The time of the full moon was coming near. The moon had been our friend during the long winter, giving us light to hunt by for a week or two each month. Now it seemed no longer a friend, but something to be regarded with fear.

We awoke early on April 3 and again traveled for ten hours. As the daylight was

now continuous, we could travel as long as we pleased and sleep as little as we must.

We slept only a few hours that night, leaving camp again a little before midnight.

We traveled for ten hours, the dogs often on the trot and sometimes running. A sledge runner passed over my foot when I stumbled while running beside a team, but the injury did not stop me.

That night [April 4] I wrote in my diary: "Give me three more days of this weather." The temperature had been minus 40 degrees. I had not dared to hope for such progress as we were making. Still the biting cold would have been impossible to face by anyone not filled with my strong purpose.

We were the only living things in a white, cold desert of ice. I knew that there was a possibility that we might end our lives there.

We had been fortunate so far, but I was in dread of finding a lead we could not cross when we came near our goal. On the 5th of April I gave the party a little more sleep as we were all badly in need of a rest. My instruments showed we were thirty-five miles from the Pole.

On April 6 we were at the end of the last long march of our journey. Yet with the Pole actually in sight I was too weary to take

the last few steps. I turned in for a few hours of absolutely necessary sleep.

I could not sleep long. The first thing I did upon awakening was to write these words in my diary: "The Pole at last! The prize of three centuries. My dream and goal for twenty years. I cannot bring myself to realize it."

We planted five flags at the top of the world. I had an American flag which I had carried wrapped around my body on every one of my expeditions. At the point farthest north on each of my expeditions, I had left a part of it. A strip of it now lies at the North Pole.

After I had planted another American flag in the ice, I told the Americans and the Eskimos to give three cheers, and I then shook hands with each member of the party. Then, in a space between the ice blocks, I put a glass bottle containing a piece of the flag I had carried around my body and this record:

> *90 N. Lat., North Pole*
> *April 6, 1909*
>
> *Arrived here today, 27 marches from C. Columbia. I have with me 5 men. My ship is in winter quarters 90 miles east of Cape Columbia.*
>
> *The expedition under my command which has succeeded in reaching the Pole is under the auspices of the Peary Arctic Club of New York City, and has been fitted out and sent North by the members and friends of the club for the honor and prestige of the United States of America.*
>
> *I start back for Cape Columbia tomorrow.*
>
> *Robert E. Peary,*
> *United States Navy*

> *90 N. Lat., North Pole*
> *April 6, 1909*
>
> *I have today hoisted the national ensign of the United States of America at this place, which my observations indicate to be the North Polar axis of the earth, and have formally taken possession of the entire region for and in the name of the President of the United States of America.*
>
> *I leave this record and the United States flag in possession.*
>
> *Robert E. Peary,*
> *United States Navy*

Roald Amundsen

*Discoverer of the South Pole
— in 1911*

You will remember that all of the explorers you have read about so far have found other human beings almost every place they went. In all recorded history only one continent has been discovered in the sense that the explorers who reported it were the first human beings to stand on its shore. That continent is Antarctica.

Roald Amundsen, a Norwegian, first reached the South Pole in 1911. Captain Robert Scott, an Englishman, was attempting to reach it at the same time. Amundsen tells us why he thinks he was successful and Scott was not:

> Our choice of a site for our base camp on the barrier [an extension of the antarctic ice sheet into the seas, resting partly on the bottom] was an essential factor in our

success. Scott's choice of a site on the mainland to the west was an essential factor in his inability to return in safety from the Pole. In the first place, the air currents in the Antarctic regions make the weather much more severe on the land than on the ice. Our camp on the ice had much better weather and at no time were we uncomfortable.

Another thing which was most essential to our success was our use of dogs. The reason briefly is this: Our method of attacking the Pole was to make repeated trips from the permanent camp southward, setting up shelters and leaving stores of food one after the other at several days' travel apart. This meant that we could make our trip to the Pole without having to carry all our supplies for the return trip. We set up these shelters very quickly. At each one we left the minimum weight of supplies for the return trip. I also planned to use our dogs as part of our food supply. There is about fifty pounds of edible food in the carcass of an Eskimo dog. I figured that as a dog's usefulness for drawing sleds ended we would use it for food.

Scott and his companions died on their return from the Pole, not from broken hearts over our earlier arrival, but from actual starvation, because of their inability to provide adequately for food on their return trip.

The rest of what happened is a familiar story. With four companions, I reached the South Pole in December, 1911, and camped there for three days. We then explored the area of our camp within a radius of ten miles, to make certain that we set foot on the actual site of the Pole. We left the Norwegian flag and the records of our observations in a tent at the Pole and returned safely to our camp.

A month later, in January, 1912, Scott arrived at the Pole and found these records. Scott and his four companions made a gallant effort to return to their base camp, but perished of starvation and exposure before they could reach it.

———

Since Hannu, our first explorer, went to the east coast of Africa, man has ranged east, west, north, and south over the face of his planet. In our own century he has begun to explore in two other directions, up and down. The United States and Russia have led in the exploration of space, and the men who have been highest above the earth are Americans and Russians.

Yuri Gagarin

*Spaceman who orbited
the earth — in 1961*

Yuri Gagarin was the first man to circle the earth in a satellite space ship. On April 12, 1961, his ship left Russia and was in orbit for 89 minutes of a 108-minute trip. The rest of the time was spent in climbing into orbit and returning to earth. The speed of the space ship was over 17,000 miles an hour—the fastest that man had ever traveled. Gagarin also flew higher (188 miles) than man had ever flown before. American news sources reported Gagarin's account of his flight:

During the boost stage of the flight I was not disturbed by the speed, the vibration, or noise. I was able to work. Once I was in orbit, and separated from the carrier rocket, I experienced weightlessness. At first the sensation was unusual, but I became used to it and was able to carry out the program we had planned.

Weightlessness makes everything easier to do. One's legs and arms weigh nothing. Objects float in the cabin. I did not sit in my chair, as before, but hung in mid-air. While in the state of weightlessness, I ate and drank. Everything happened just as it does on earth. I worked well in that condition. I wrote, jotting down my observations. My handwriting did not change, although my hand did not weigh anything. But I had to hold the notebook, otherwise it would have

floated away. I was in constant radio contact with the earth.

From a height of 188 miles, the earth has a very beautiful blue halo. At the horizon a gradual change in colors takes place, from soft blue light to dark blue, from dark blue to violet, and then to black. The change is very smooth and very beautiful. The entrance into the earth's shadow happens very quickly. [It was night on the Western Hemisphere when Gagarin crossed it.] One goes from light to darkness, and on the dark side of the earth, nothing at all is visible. I could see the shores, islands, rivers, and oceans on the daytime side of the earth very well. When I came out of the shadow of the earth, the halo was a different color. At the horizon one could see a bright orange which then became all colors of the rainbow on the rest of the surface. The sky remained black.

I did not see the moon. The sun in outer space is ten times brighter than here on earth. The stars are very bright, and are colored red, white, and yellow.

I passed the Antarctic, Cape Horn, Central Africa, the Mediterranean, the Balkans —and then I saw Russia.

I was the first man ever to see with my own eyes the spherical shape of the earth.

Jacques Piccard

*Explorer who reached the
deepest spot of the ocean
floor, and published
findings — in 1960–1961*

The task of mapping the land surface of the earth
is almost finished. But about three-fourths of the
earth is covered with water. It is only in our own
century that men have been able to live and move
beneath the ocean surface for more than a few
minutes at a time. The deepest spot in the ocean
is believed to be nearly 36,800 feet, or about seven
miles, down. Man first reached this depth in 1960
when the Swiss Jacques Piccard and the American
submarine Lieutenant Don Walsh went down in a
bathyscaphe. *Bathyscaphe* means "deep boat." The
bathyscaphe was invented by Piccard's father.

The United States Navy was in charge of this
exploration. It took place near the island of Guam
in the Pacific Ocean. Here the ocean bed is cracked
with a trench far deeper than the Grand Canyon.
It took Piccard from about eight o'clock in the morn-

ing to about four o'clock in the afternoon to go down seven miles to the bottom of the trench and to return to the surface. The following account is from Jacques Piccard's book, *Seven Miles Down:*

At 800 feet down, we began to drop in earnest. We had passed the sea's twilight zone. Beyond the port [plastic window] there was darkness, but not yet total blackness. Descending into the sea, the night comes slowly like a northern evening.

At 1,000 feet I turned off the cabin light for a careful look into the sea. A little light still seeped down from above. I turned the cabin light on again. I tested the forward beam that throws light into the sea. It picked up plankton, a simple form of sea life. With our light on it, it looked like snowfall— only, since we were going down, it streamed upward instead of downward.

We were going at the speed of the average elevator, three feet per second. We spoke to men on the boat above on a special telephone. It was pleasant to hear voices from above. Why, I don't know. We are now far beyond the reach of help.

There was a very real danger. The charts had warned me that the canyon into which we were falling was only one mile wide at the bottom. It was possible that we might collide with the wall of the canyon—a chilling thought!

2,400 feet. Outside, total blackness. We dimmed our cabin light, leaving only enough light to read our instruments. We wanted our eyes to adapt to the darkness. Inside the sphere we could feel the chill of the water. Both Walsh and I had been thoroughly soaked with water while preparing for the dive. Now it was time to change into dry clothing—no simple task in our cell less than six feet high with only three feet between the instruments.

We broke out our first chocolate bars— the only food aboard. Walsh and I had a private joke about these "lunches." On the last dive I had provided lunch—Swiss chocolate bars. This time Walsh offered to bring the lunch. He did—fifteen American chocolate bars.

We continued to plunge. Black water rushed upward past us. We went beyond record depths that we had reached earlier. At 20,000 feet we were at maximum normal sea floor, and we began to drop into the canyon. Only one per cent of the ocean bottom has trenches like this one, whose bottoms are below 20,000 feet.

29,150 feet. We were now as deep under the sea as the highest mountain is high above it. The water was clear, with none of the "sea snow" of plankton. There was perhaps a mile of water still beneath us, but the possibility of hitting the canyon wall was still on my mind. I pushed a button, slowing us down to two feet per second; then, to one foot per second.

Just before one o'clock in the afternoon, Walsh said, "There it is, Jacques! It looks like we have found it!" Yes, we were finally near the bottom.

While I looked through the port, Walsh called out the distances to the bottom and we continued to fall: "Twenty — 18 — 15. Going right down. Six — we're slowing up, very slowly, we may come to a stop. You say you saw a small animal, possibly a red shrimp about one inch long? Wonderful, wonderful! You can see the bottom through the port? Good — we've made it!" Slowly, Walsh and I shook hands.

Jacques-Yves Cousteau

Inventor of the aqualung
who experimented with
an underwater room — in 1962

If man can learn to live in the ocean, the day will come when he will raise fish as he now raises cows and pigs. We will have mines in the ocean floor and bring up minerals. A French explorer has done much to make it possible for man to live in water. Jacques-Yves Cousteau has been called the "Father of Free Diving." He helped invent the aqualung which makes it possible for man to carry his air supply into the sea with him.

Cousteau explored the Atlantic, the Mediterranean, the Caribbean, and the Red Sea. With the help of other scientists, he has mapped many of the mountains, valleys, cliffs and sloping beds that make up the ocean floor. Here he writes about an experiment with another way of observing life in the ocean. In the Mediterranean, near Marseilles, France, he and his helpers set up an underwater room on the continental shelf. (The continental shelf is actually a part of a continent that is under water. The water above the shelf is not so deep as is the rest of the ocean.) In Continental Shelf Station Number One (Conshelf One), two men lived for a week without ever coming to the surface of the water. In a book, *The Living Sea*, Cousteau describes this underwater room:

Conshelf One was centered around a cylindrical dwelling and workshop seventeen feet long and eight feet high, anchored with eight chains seven feet above a floor forty feet deep. It was a halfway house that permitted the divers to work in the open water eighty feet down.

On the bottom of the chamber there was a hatch always open to the sea, which was kept down by internal air pressure. Through their liquid door the divers passed in and out to perform labors that anticipated those of workers in the continental-shelf stations of tomorrow.

Falco and Wesly entered Conshelf One on September 14, 1962. We watched them settling into their quarters on a television set in a house on the nearby shore. We knew everything about them as soon as it occurred. We heard every word and noise. They were to be visited twice daily by two doctors.

During the first afternoon I swam down to Conshelf One and found the men in lofty form. They were excited by the water encompassing them, by the easy way into it, by the long periods they could spend outside in the water and by the comforts of the station. They had a television set bringing in the national network, a radio, a library, and even an abstract painting by Laban. They had a hot fresh-water shower piped through a plastic tube from a boat on the surface. Their meals were sent down in pressure cookers. There was an electric stove to rewarm food or to cook it should meal delivery be interrupted. Above, there were sixty men to look after them.

On the second night, our motion picture cameraman went down with ten assistants to film the men on the continental shelf. From the boat I looked through the clear water at the big yellow chamber bathed in floodlight. I could see the exhaust bubbles boiling out of the station. Around the Conshelf area floodlights came on and signal lights blinked as the cameraman positioned them to film Falco and Wesly. There appeared a new dazzle of lights in a row leading down a slope on the ocean floor. I decided to descend and have a look.

I donned my diving gear and plunged. In the illuminated acres of Conshelf, the cameraman and his assistants hovered like shadows,

concentrating lights on Falco and Wesly, who were swimming side-by-side down the radiant boulevard. The pair was moving easily as if their rubber fins were a natural part of the feet.

They swam down the beam of light across sand and past sea cucumbers, toward the open sea beyond the lights. The cameraman signaled and all the lights went out. The film sequence was finished; the cameramen had to return. I was able to linger awhile after the film team had surfaced. In the darkness all that I could see was two wands of light as Falco and Wesly moved along lightly touching the fish with blue gloves. They stopped and petted a cuttlefish, unaware that anyone was watching.

I hung forsaken in the night, full of thoughts. My life's work had been to free man from the surface, permit him to escape beyond natural limits, to breathe in water, and to resist ever-increasing pressures. And not only to put man there but to help him to adapt, explore, subsist, survive, and learn. Now he was beginning to live in the ocean, of the ocean, and for the ocean in the person of these two men.

CONTRASTING MAN'S IDEAS

Thousands of years ago man believed that his world was flat and was surrounded by a salt-water river. One of the wheel maps showing this belief is shown. Study this map and tell some of ancient man's ideas of his world.

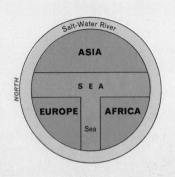

John Glenn, Jr., was the first American to orbit the earth on February 20, 1962. The modern map shows the paths of the three orbits he made during his flight. How has map information changed between the days of the wheel map and the 1962 map? Contrast the ideas of ancient man and modern man as shown on the two maps.

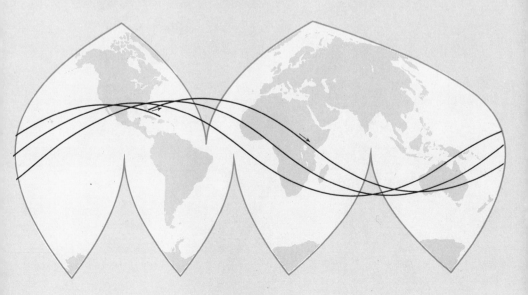

MAPPING THE WORLD

In Unit Three you have crossed the oceans to every continent. You have traveled to the poles, orbited into space, and plunged to great depths beneath the sea. There are still many places which are unexplored: mountain peaks, interiors of continents, planets, under the sea, and so on. Cartographers (map and chart makers) will continue to change the mapping of the earth, ocean, and space with the assistance of many other experts. Pictures of some of these experts are in the illustrations which follow. Discuss the part these people play in mapping the earth. You will probably find that you need more information to discuss cartography accurately.

KNOWING WORD MEANINGS

1. Context Clues, Glossary, and Dictionary

How effective were you in determining the meanings and the pronunciation of the words used in Unit Three? Did you use the context clues whenever possible and then check with the Glossary to be sure you were correct? Did you use the Glossary or the dictionary for meanings of words not explained by context?

Pronounce and give the meanings of the following words as they are used in this unit. How did you arrive at your decision? If you used the context, turn to the page listed and read the clue, or clues, which gave you your information. If there was more than one definition in the Glossary or dictionary, tell how you decided which one to use.

Page 95, translated   *Page 139*, perished
Page 98, Archipelago   *Page 153*, colors
Page 104, far-fetched *Page 164*, cast
Page 110, altered   *Page 168*, qualify
Page 114, parchment   *Page 174*, lead
Page 123, standard   *Page 178*, ensign
Page 127, doldrums   *Page 181*, gallant
Page 133, pacifying   *Page 184*, halo

2. Structure Clues

a. Compound Words

Give the meaning of the following compound words. Tell whether the meaning of the smaller words has been kept or whether the compound word has a new meaning.

Page 98, hearsay   *Page 120*, underestimated
Page 116, mankind   *Page 128*, outlast

Page 132, stowaway   *Page 157*, overland
Page 134, hardships   *Page 193*, floodlight

b. Words, Prefixes, and Suffixes

Prefixes and suffixes added to root words make two changes in the new form. The meaning is changed and the way the word is used in the sentence is changed. What does just mean in this sentence and how is it used?

Leif Ericson was a just man.

You are correct if you said that Leif was fair, or honorable, and that *just* described man. You could have said that *just* was used as an adjective.

Read the following sentences. For how many of the underlined words can you give the meaning and tell how they are used in the sentences? If you need to, use the Glossary or the dictionary.

1. Las Casas believed in justice for the Indians.

2. A great injustice was done Columbus by a German map maker.

3. Cook tried to treat the natives justly.

4. Balboa was accused unjustly of treason.

5. Amundsen could justify his use of dogs for food.

6. All the fears of Vasco da Gama's seamen were not justified.

7. Was Magellan's death justifiable?

8. Piccard and Walsh were justifiably proud of their deep-sea dive.

3. Word History—Descriptive Names

The mystery of the unknown has always tempted men to seek new horizons. Each new discovery has usually added new words to the language. Actually the explorations of men can often be traced by studying the language used for place names.

In Unit Three many of the place names were chosen because the discoverer wanted to describe the area he had found.

The early Romans called the Mediterranean the *Inner Sea* to contrast it with their name for the Atlantic Ocean, which was the *Outer Sea*. It was only after much exploration that the word Mediterranean was used.

Several of the continents seem to have been given descriptive names. Some people believe that the word *Asia* means *east* and that *Europe* means the opposite, or *west*. The word *Europe* has been traced by some scholars to mean *broad land*, because it was wider from east to west than it was from north to south. Other people think that the name Europe came from *Europa*, the name of the sister of a man who is thought to have brought the alphabet to Greece from Phoenicia. *Australia* comes from Latin, and means *south wind* or *south land*.

Some of the oceans had descriptive names, too. The Pacific Ocean was given its name by Magellan, because during his voyage to the Philippines it was so calm and peaceful. *Arctic* comes from Greek and means both *north* and *bear*. This was because of the North Star in the constellation which we know as the Little Dipper, but which earlier people called the Little Bear. *Antarctic* means *opposite the north*.

It would seem that the Canary Islands were named because of the large number of canaries found on the islands. Actually the opposite is true. Columbus, on his second voyage to the New World, was impressed by the great number of wild dogs on these islands. He used the Latin word *canis* meaning *dog* to name these islands "Dog Islands." Can you see how *canis* after many centuries would become *canary?* The birds were then named after the islands.

We continue to use descriptive words today for new ideas, events, or discoveries. *Astronaut,* meaning "sailor to the stars," is one of these new words. This word will not be found in most of the dictionaries which have a copyright date earlier than 1960.

Our language will keep on growing as long as there is a need for new words to describe something. Many of these words will be taken from other languages.

Use your encyclopedia and find at least one state, county, and city in the United States which has a descriptive name. What does each name mean and from what language did it come?

UNIT FOUR
Reading to Form Mental Images

SEEING AND HEARING THROUGH WORDS

Much of your knowledge comes to you from actual experiences. When you see a rainbow or hear a song, you are using your senses of sight or sound. But how do you obtain knowledge of experiences which other people have had? Words can help you imagine those experiences and BUILD MENTAL IMAGES. Words can help you see the earth from a height of 188 miles, or see the court of Kublai Khan. Through words you can hear the voice of Vasco da Gama speaking to his men as he threw all the instruments into the sea, or the battle between Magellan's men and the Indians. Your mind translates the words you have read to a mental image, and you often think that you have had the real experience.

More than 165 years ago, Samuel Taylor Coleridge wrote a poem called "The Rime of the Ancient Mariner." People have been enjoying his poem ever since. One of the reasons they enjoy it is that they can see and hear what the mariner (or sailor) saw and heard. Several stanzas from this poem have been selected for you to read.

See a sailing ship that cannot move because there is no breeze on a hot day.

All in a hot and copper sky
The bloody sun, at noon,
Right up above the mast did stand
No bigger than the moon.

Day after day, day after day,
We stuck, nor breath nor motion:
As idle as a painted ship
Upon a painted ocean.

See the icebergs in a polar region.

And now there came both mist and snow,
And it grew wondrous cold;
And ice, mast-high, came floating by
As green as emerald.

Hear the huge icebergs grinding together.

The ice was here, the ice was there,
The ice was all around:
It cracked and growled and roared and
    howled
Like noises in a swound.

Do you know what "Like noises in a swound" means? *Swound* is an old word which is no longer used. It may not be in your dictionary. Swound means *faint*. People sometimes report that they have heard unusual noises just before they fainted. Now, tell what you think "Like noises in a swound" means.

The interesting thing is that you may have known what the poetry meant even if you did not know all the words. You saw and heard what the poet, Coleridge, wanted you to see and hear, because many of his words appeal to the senses.

Coleridge used "painted ocean" and "ice mast-high" to appeal to your sense of sight. What other words or phrases can you find in the stanzas which describe sights?

What words did Coleridge use to describe sound?

USING OTHER SENSES AS YOU READ

You are probably more aware of the senses of sight and sound than of any others. Smell, taste, and touch are the other three senses people think of when they speak of the five senses. Yet there are many more. There is a sense of pain, of hunger, and of thirst. The sense of weight, as well as the sense of touch, is involved when you hold an object in your hand. The sense of temperature is one Coleridge used in the lines you have just read. Reread the four stanzas. What words did Coleridge use to describe temperature?

Words can stir your sense of motion or lack of motion. What imaginary experiences do you have as you read these lines about the ship?

Day after day, day after day,
We stuck, nor breath nor motion;

Then like a pawing horse let go,
She made a sudden bound;
It flung the blood into my head,
And I fell down into a swound.

Swiftly, swiftly flew the ship
Yet she sailed softly too;
Sweetly, sweetly blew the breeze —
On me alone it blew.

Experience the thirst of the sailors whose supply of drinking water has run out.

Water, water everywhere
And all the boards did shrink;
Water, water everywhere
Nor any drop to drink.

Have you ever seen the sea from so great a height that the waves looked like wrinkles? In the poem which follows, what words or phrases give you a feeling of great height? Check the glossary for the meaning of "crag" and "azure" before you start to read the poem.

The Eagle

He clasps the crag with crooked hands;
Close to the sun in lonely lands,
Ringed with the azure world, he stands.

The wrinkled sea beneath him crawls;
He watches from his mountain walls,
And like a thunderbolt he falls.

Alfred, Lord Tennyson

Often one word will appeal to several senses. *Ice* appeals to the sense of sight and to the sense of temperature. We can SEE water, yet "Water, water everywhere, Nor any drop to drink," also appeals strongly to our sense of THIRST. If one word gives us several sense impressions, so much the better.

In real life, you are not aware of each sense separately. If you think of what your senses are telling you about the place you are sitting now, you will find sights, sounds, and smells are mingled. The sight of your desk, the temperature of the room, the sound of students talking, your own hunger — these all blend together. In the same way, Coleridge makes us feel the cold, see the ice, and hear icebergs grinding together, all at the same time.

If you read "with your senses," books can help you to do things you have never done, to see things you have never seen, and to go places where you may never go.

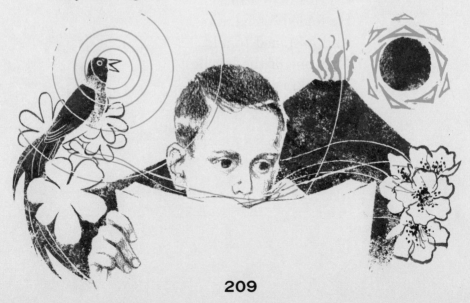

Several senses are appealed to in this poem.
What are they?

The Meal

Timothy Tompkins had turnips
  and tea.
The turnips were tiny.
He ate at least three.
And then, for dessert,
He had onions and ice.
He liked that so much
That he ordered it twice.
He had two cups of ketchup,
A prune, and a pickle.
"Delicious," said Timothy.
"Well worth a nickel."
He folded his napkin
And hastened to add,
"It's one of the loveliest
  breakfasts I've had."

Karla Kuskin

Most of the next poem deals with visual images, but at least five of its descriptions of white stir other senses beside the sense of sight. Can you find five descriptions of white that appeal to senses other than the sense of sight?

What Is White?

White is a dove
And a lily of the valley
And a puddle of milk
Spilled in an alley —
A ship's sail
A kite's tail
A wedding veil
Hailstones and
Halibut bones
And some people's
Telephones.
The hottest and most blinding light
Is white.
And breath is white
When you blow it out on a frosty night.
White is the shining absence of all color
Then absence is white
Out of touch
Out of sight.

White is marshmallow
and vanilla ice cream
And the part you can't remember
In a dream.
White is the sound
Of a light foot walking
White is a pair of
Whispers talking.
White is the beautiful
Broken lace
Of snowflakes falling
On your face.
You can smell white
In a country room
Toward the end of May
In the cherry bloom.

Mary O'Neill

The next six lines are from a poem by Vachel Lindsay. The poet's words should appeal to at least four of your senses. What are they? What words in these lines appeal to several senses?

Last night at black midnight I woke
  with a cry,
The windows were shaking, there was
  thunder on high,
The floor was atremble, the door
  was ajar,
White fires, crimson fires, shone
  from afar.
I rushed to the dooryard. The city
  was gone.
My home was a hut without orchard
  or lawn.

What disastrous thing has happened? Did you think that a bomb had fallen, or that there had been an earthquake? Would you be surprised to know that the title of the poem is "The Ghost of the Buffaloes"? Does knowing the title change your sensations of fright, sound, motion, or sight? Your mental images are probably the same, but your concept of the event itself has changed because of your knowledge of the title.

USING ALL THE READING RULES

As you grow in the ability to build mental images, you will understand more of what you read. You will also get more pleasure from your reading.

REMEMBER
SPEED
DETAILS
RESEARCH
CONCENTRATE
WORD MEANING
PURPOSE
RELATIONSHIPS
BUILD MENTAL IMAGES

In order to build mental images you need to use all of the reading rules. Reread the rules on page 13. Then use as a guide the shortened form of each rule on page 214, and tell how you apply the rules as you learn to BUILD BETTER MENTAL IMAGES.

READING PROSE AND FORMING MENTAL IMAGES

Poetry appeals to the senses, but prose does too. Do you know the difference between poetry and prose? Poetry often rhymes and usually has a regular rhythm. Prose is closer to everyday speech.

The following prose description of Ichabod Crane contains many visual images. Ichabod is a character in a story written by Washington Irving. Look for the meanings of "snipe" and "spindle neck" in the Glossary before you start to read. After you have read the description, draw a sketch of Ichabod.

He was tall, but exceedingly lank, with narrow shoulders, long arms and legs, hands that dangled a mile out of his sleeves, feet that might have served for shovels, and his whole frame most loosely hung together. His head was small and flat at top, with huge ears, large green glassy eyes, and a long snipe nose, so that it looked like a weathercock perched upon his spindle neck to tell which way the wind blew.

Compare your sketch with those of your classmates. Are the sketches alike? If all of you had the same mental image, it would be unusual. You all read the same words, but words can build different mental images for different people.

E. B. White's book *Charlotte's Web* has this description of a barn (the home of Wilbur, the pig). What senses are appealed to in this prose?

The barn was very large. It was very old. It smelled of hay and it smelled of manure. It smelled of the perspiration of tired horses and the wonderful sweet breath of patient cows. It often had a sort of peaceful smell — as though nothing bad could happen ever again in the world. It smelled of grain and of harness dressing and of axle grease and of rubber boots and of new rope. And whenever the cat was given a fish-head to eat, the barn would smell of fish. But mostly it smelled of hay, for there was always hay in the great loft up overhead. And there was always hay being pitched down to the cows and the horses and the sheep.

The barn was pleasantly warm in winter when the animals spent most of their time indoors, and it was pleasantly cool in summer when the big doors stood wide open to the breeze. The barn had stalls on the main floor for the work horses, tie-ups on the main floor for the cows, a sheepfold down below for the sheep, a pigpen down below for Wilbur, and it was full of all sorts of things that you find in barns: ladders, grindstones, pitch forks, monkey wrenches, scythes, lawn mowers, snow shovels, ax handles, milk pails, water buckets, empty grain sacks, and rusty rat traps. It was the kind of barn that swallows like to build their nests in. It was the kind of barn that children like to play in.

You may not have seen some of the things that were in Wilbur's barn. Coleridge never saw the polar region, yet he could describe it. Perhaps he talked to sailors who had been there. Maybe he read a book about the cold icy regions. We are sure that he knew the meanings of many words and used those words well to stir your imagination.

See if you can write a description of one thing you have never seen which was in Wilbur's barn. Why will you need to get information from other sources and know the meanings of the words you use? Share your description with your classmates.

The following paragraph is taken from the book *The House of Sixty Fathers* by Meindert DeJong. Several of your senses will be appealed to in this paragraph. As you read the paragraph, list as many of these senses as you can. Tell which words stir each sense.

In the late afternoon Tien Pao suddenly could go no farther. He broke into a cold sweat, his legs trembled under him, he was nauseated with hunger. He had reached the top of a round, grassy hill. There were a few sheltering bushes, and he crawled behind them. He had to eat, had to rest. He dug his hand into the rice bowl and gulped a choking big mouthful. Glory-of-the-Republic [Tien Pao's pet pig] began tearing at the grass. Tien Pao dug his hand into the bowl again, stuffed his mouth full. Again his hand went to the bowl. He pulled it back. There was only a good handful of rice left in the bottom of the bowl. He mustn't touch it, mustn't eat it — he mustn't keep looking at it! It had to be saved for one more meal.

Compare your list with the lists of your classmates. Of course your lists will not be alike. Why are they not the same? Several people can read the same paragraph, but the words in that paragraph may stir different senses in each person. The mental images for different people are not the same.

Building mental images as you read science and social studies will help you understand and enjoy books you read. What senses are appealed to in this paragraph about the ameba?

The ameba is a strange, jelly-like animal which has no definite shape. It is so small that many thousands can live in one drop of water. The ameba reproduces in a simple way. It merely divides itself. If it has enough food and the right living conditions, it will divide into two amebas in about an hour. In less than another hour these two amebas will divide into four. Before the end of the fourth hour, sixteen. If this process of division continued, there would be one pound of amebas at the end of two days. By the end of the sixth day the amebas would weigh more than the earth itself!

The next paragraph about an event in the life of Alexander the Great has many words to help you experience this battle in imagination. What words appeal to which senses?

Across the river Alexander could see his enemies, the Persians. His generals begged him not to attack until the next morning. But Alexander decided to open the battle at once and take the enemy by surprise.

He called for his horse and gave the order for the trumpets to sound.

"Onward! Onward!" the men shouted the battle cry. They were calling to their god of war to give them victory. Alexander, with his spear raised, started across the shallow river at the head of his army.

The enemy hurled loads of red-hot sand on the attacking army. Fire darts and spears came flying through the air. Fighting desperately, Alexander and his army reached the opposite shore.

There the full force of the enemy met the invaders. A Persian soldier raised his spear to kill Alexander. But the king's faithful guard struck off the man's arm with his sword. Still later Alexander's helmet was pierced and blood poured from a wound in his head. Alexander only laughed and went on fighting. No one could resist him and his army.

Gradually the Persians gave ground. At last their entire army was in retreat. By the time the sun had slipped behind the hills, the battle was over. Alexander had done what many believed to be impossible. He had put to flight the greatest army in the world.

USING WORDS TO COMPARE

Writers try to help you understand their ideas by using special forms of comparison. Tennyson compared the downward flight of the eagle to a thunderbolt. Washington Irving compared Ichabod Crane's head to a weathercock. These comparisons are called similes. The words *like* and *as* help you to recognize similes when you are reading. You often use similes in your daily speech. You might say: "This room is *as* cold *as* ice," or "The clown cried *like* a baby."

Coleridge made use of a simile to describe the ship when it begins to move:

"Then *like* a pawing horse let go
She made a sudden bound."

What is the simile in this poem?

Taxis
Ho, for taxis green or blue,
Hi, for taxis red,
They roll along the Avenue
Like spools of colored thread!

Rachel Field

What similes can you find in this paragraph from the book *Farmer Boy* by Laura Ingalls Wilder?

Mother was short and plump and pretty. Her eyes were blue, and her brown hair was like a bird's smooth wings. A row of little red buttons ran down the front of her dress of wine-colored wool, from her flat white linen collar to the white apron tied round her waist. Her big sleeves hung like large red bells at either end of the blue platter.

A SIMILE always has the words *like* or *as*. But look at the first line of Tennyson's "The Eagle":
"He clasps the crag with crooked hands"
Does an eagle have hands? You can guess that what is meant is, "He clasps the crag with feet *like* crooked hands." This line of poetry from "The Eagle" contains a metaphor.

A METAPHOR is a comparison without the words *like* or *as*. A "snowy shirt" is a metaphor; "a shirt as white as snow" is a simile. Metaphors and similes are used by writers to show comparisons.

Read the following sentences. Which sentence uses a metaphor to compare? a simile?

1. She has cold hands.
2. Her hands are as cold as ice.
3. Her icy hands made me shiver.

See if you can make the following statements more interesting by using similes or metaphors.

1. The racing car is fast.
2. The explorer was brave.
3. The sea was calm.

In this poem about the wind, a metaphor is the basis of the poem. What is the metaphor? There is also a simile in the poem. What is it?

Wind Is a Cat

Wind is a cat
That prowls at night,
Now in a valley,
Now on a height.

Pouncing on houses
Till folks in their beds
Draw all the covers
Over their heads.

It sings to the moon
It scratches at doors;
It lashes its tail
Around chimneys and roars.

It claws at the clouds
Till it fringes their silk;
It laps up the dawn
Like a saucer of milk;

Then, chasing the stars
To the top of the firs,
Curls down for a nap
And purrs and purrs.

Ethel Romig Fuller

As you read the next poem, look for a simile and a metaphor. According to the poet's words, what is a sea shell? What are echoes like? Which is the simile? the metaphor?

Palace

A sea shell is a palace
Where many echoes dwell,
And when I listen to them
I know them all quite well.
They are like the ocean's roar
Where the sea shell buried deep
Learns why the sea is always salt,
And spooky shadows creep.

Dorothy Vena Johnson

Writers make use of similes and metaphors to help you understand their ideas and build mental images. These images can make you sense something you never sensed before, or sense things more clearly than ever before. Images can help you understand something you never understood before, or never understood so clearly.

MAKING WRITING MORE EFFECTIVE

The numbered sentences which follow are alike in meaning, but the word order has been changed in sentence number two. The usual word order, or pattern, of sentences is to name the subject first and then the verb. Then words or phrases which describe either the subject or the verb are added. Read the following sentences. Which sentence appeals more quickly to your senses?

1. A grizzled pirate sneaked stealthily across the deck in the darkness.
2. Stealthily across the deck in the darkness sneaked a grizzled pirate.

Many people feel that the word order of the second sentence gives them a more vivid picture of the pirate's actions. When the writer placed the words "stealthily," "across the deck," "in the darkness," and "sneaked," *before* the subject of the sentence, he helped you sense immediately the mood of the situation.

Writers of prose often choose to use a different word order in their sentences to provide variety in their writing. They often wish to use a more effective style of writing which they hope will help you have a better understanding of their ideas. They may want to set the mood, or to stress an important point by changing the word order of their sentences.

The writer of the next prose selection has changed the usual word order in several sentences. As you read, look for sentences which have a changed word order. Read them aloud. Choose three of these sentences and rewrite them using the usual word order or sentence pattern. Be sure that the subject comes first and then the verb.

Compare your sentences with those of the author of "Success Story," which follows. Which sentences are more effective, the author's or yours? Why?

All was quiet on board the small ship. The only light came from a thin crescent moon which was far down on the horizon. Stealthily across the deck in the darkness sneaked a grizzled pirate. Cautiously he glanced around the ship, looking for possible opposition. A shadowy form at the wheel was the only human being in sight. Confident of his escape now and moving quietly, the pirate neared the portside. Suddenly out of nowhere came the sound of running feet. The pirate turned quickly to defend himself, but John was already grabbing him. Roaring with anger the pirate tried to break John's grip of iron. The noise of the struggle had brought John's sleepy companions on deck. Wide awake now and realizing the danger, John's shipmates rushed to help him subdue the pirate.

The curtain went down amid thunderous applause. The cast of Libertyville's spring play knew that their hard work and long hours of practice had really paid off. The play was a success.

Poets often use an unusual word order when they wish to maintain a certain pattern of rhyme and rhythm. They, too, wish to make their poetry more effective and to develop their own style of writing. Coleridge was writing about a very hot day, and wanted you to imagine what it was like. He changed the word order of his lines when he wrote:

"All in a hot and copper sky,
The bloody sun, at noon,
Right up above the mast did stand,
No bigger than the moon."

How does changed word order in the next poem make the writing more effective? What mental images are stimulated as you read the poem? What is the simile?

Up in the Air
Zooming across the sky
Like a great bird you fly,
Airplane,
Silvery white
In the light.

Turning and twisting in air,
When shall I ever be there,
    Airplane,
    Piloting you
    Far in the blue?

James S. Tippett

Many people enjoy reading, writing, and listening to limericks. A limerick is a humorous five-line verse. As you read the following limerick, notice how the changed word order made the limerick funny.

Point of View

As a beauty I am not a star,
There are others more handsome, by far,
    But my face — I don't mind it
    Because I'm behind it;
It's the people in front get the jar!

CHANGING WORD ORDER
FOR UNDERSTANDING

Rewriting of poetry into prose, which changes the word order of the lines, often makes the words less effective. But it is one way to see if you understand the poetry.

A student rewrote the poem "To Beachey, 1912" by Carl Sandburg:

The plane purrs as it flies east. The plane and the pilot seem to be blended into one thing. The pilot sits with his hands on the wheel. He loves to be in the air. The wings of the plane are helping to keep the pilot safe.

Now read Mr. Sandburg's poem. Notice his choice of words and the word order of his lines. Why is Mr. Sandburg's writing more effective than the student's writing?

To Beachey, 1912

Riding against the east,
A veering, steady shadow
Purrs the motor-call
Of the man-bird
Ready with the death-laughter
In his throat
And in his heart always
The love of the big blue beyond.

Only a man,
A far fleck of shadow on the east
Sitting at ease
With his hands on a wheel
And around him the large gray wings.
Hold him, great soft wings,
Keep and deal kindly, O wings,
With the cool, calm shadow at the wheel.

There are many ways of thinking about the wind. A scientist wants to know certain facts about it and uses instruments to measure such factors as speed or direction. A poet usually is not trying to tell you facts. He is trying to get you to share an experience.

You cannot see the wind, so the poet who wrote the next poem had to use words which stir other senses to describe it. What words are used to help you build mental images of the wind?

Knowing the meaning of the words in "The Wind's Visit" is very important if you are going to understand this poem. As you read it, decide which words you need to look up in the glossary. Reread the poem. How does the writer's choice of words help you understand how she sees the wind?

The Wind's Visit

The wind tapped like a tired man,
And like a host, "Come in,"
I boldly answered; entered then
My residence within

A rapid, footless guest,
To offer whom a chair
Were as impossible as hand
A sofa to the air.

No bone had he to bind him,
His speech was like the push
Of numerous humming-birds at once
From a superior bush.

His countenance a billow,
His fingers, if he pass,
Let go a music, as of tunes
Blown tremulous in glass.

He visited, still flitting;
Then, like a timid man,
Again he tapped — 'twas flurriedly —
And I became alone.

Emily Dickinson

1. Do you think "The wind tapped like a tired man" is a good comparison? Is this comparison in "The Wind's Visit" a simile or a metaphor? How do you think of the wind?

2. Think of how poets change word order as you read the next lines. What is the subject? Try to rewrite these lines in a sentence. Change the word order to the usual sentence pattern. Does changing the poet's word order help you understand the thought? Why?

> ". . . entered then
> My residence within
> A rapid, footless guest"

3. Rewrite the last three lines of stanza three. Is the wind making a loud or a soft sound? Listen to the "sh" sound at the ends of lines two and four. How do these sounds help to give you an impression of loudness or softness?

4. What does this line mean: "His countenance a billow"?

5. Have you ever blown into a bottle to hear the sound your breath makes? If you have, and if you know the meaning of "tremulous," it will be easy for you to rewrite the last three lines in stanza four.

6. A comma and a period are the only punctuation marks in the third stanza. How many punctuation marks are there in the last stanza? When read aloud, one stanza sounds like a low steady breeze. The

other stanza sounds like a breeze starting up and dying down. Which stanza sounds like a steady breeze?

After you have read the next poem, tell whether or not you think you need to rewrite it in order to understand it. What senses are appealed to in the poem?

Sea Shell

Sea Shell, Sea Shell,
   Sing me a song, O Please!
A song of ships, and sailor men,
   And parrots, and tropical trees,

Of islands lost in the Spanish Main
Which no man ever may find again,
Of fishes and corals under the waves,
And sea horses stabled in great green caves.

Sea Shell, Sea Shell,
Sing of the things you know so well.

Amy Lowell

Two different artists have drawn pictures to illustrate the poem "Sea Shell." Why are the pictures different?

Building mental images through words can be both enjoyable and profitable for you. As you read other books, magazines, and newspapers, practice this skill. Remember that you need to use all the other rules for better reading if you want to BUILD BETTER MENTAL IMAGES.

Egyptian
Babylonian
Roman
Chinese
Mayan
Hindu—Arabic

Abacus

Arm Measure

Quipu

Sundial

I COUNT NONE BUT SUNNY HOURS

Hourglass

Reading Arithmetic

143 × 1 = 143
143 × 2 = 286
143 × 3 = 429
143 × 4 = ☐
143 × 5 = ☐
143 × 6 = ☐
143 × 7 = ☐
143 × 8 = ☐
143 × 9 = ☐

The Curious Number 143

143 × 7 = 1001
286 × 7 = 2002
429 × 7 = 3003
☐ × 7 = ☐
☐ × 7 = ☐
☐ × 7 = ☐
☐ × 7 = ☐
☐ × 7 = ☐
☐ × 7 = ☐

237

WORKING WITH SYMBOLS

Turn to the Table of Contents on page 6. Preview Unit Five by reading the titles of the eight sections in the unit. Notice that "word" appears in several titles. Your PURPOSE FOR READING this unit will be to strengthen your ability to interpret the words used in arithmetic exercises and problems.

The words of your language are symbols which communicate ideas. Unless you know the meaning of words as they are used in sentences, communication may not be accurate.

You can communicate with symbols other than words. What ideas do the following symbols communicate to you?

You also recognize the ideas communicated by the symbols used in arithmetic. When you see $+$, $-$, $\times$, or $\div$, you know that you are to add, subtract, multiply, or divide. And when you see the symbols $\frac{1}{3}$, 47, or $3.95, you know that these numerals are communicating ideas of *number* to you.

Words and number symbols are something like actors in a play. The same actor might have the part of a clown in one play and the part of a detective in another play. He would do completely different things as he played these two parts.

Numbers can play different parts, too. A number can play the part of an addend in one situation and the part of a divisor in another situation. This number would be playing completely different parts because of the words or other symbols which gave the directions.

The same numbers are used in the four problems which follow. Watch for the words which direct the part the numbers are to play. If you have forgotten the meanings of any of the words, use your arithmetic text or dictionary to refresh your memory.

1. If 19 and 6 are addends, what is the sum?
2. What is the product if 19 and 6 are the factors?
3. Find the difference between 19 and 6.
4. When the dividend is 19 and the divisor is 6, what is the quotient? the remainder?

Which word or words in each of the preceding problems told you the part that the numbers were to play?

In each of the following problems, follow the directions of the words as you work with the numbers.

1. Complete: If the product is 12 and the factors are whole numbers, the factors would be 1 and 12, or 2 and 6, or __?__ and __?__ .

2. Complete: When the dividend is 59 and the divisor is 7, the remainder is __?__ .

3. If the sum is 14 and two of the addends are 6 and 3, what is the other addend?

4. Find the dividend if the quotient is 9 and the divisor is 4. (Be careful.)

5. How much larger is the product of 3 and 7 than the sum of 3 and 7?

6. 1 and 48 are two factors of 48. What are the other factors of 48?

7. (*a*) Find the sum of 9 and 5. (*b*) Find the difference between 9 and 5. (*c*) Add the sum to the difference. (*d*) Is your answer twice the larger number given in (*a*)?

8. (*a*) What is the sum of 14 and 6? (*b*) What is the difference between 14 and 6? (*c*) Subtract the difference from the sum. (*d*) Is your answer twice the smaller number given in (*a*)?

As you can see, in these arithmetic problems it was the words which told you how to handle the numbers. KNOW THE MEANING OF EVERY WORD is a most important rule to follow when you are reading arithmetic problems.

USING WORDS TO COUNT AND MEASURE

David has this arithmetic problem to work.

> The Taylor family uses a dozen eggs a day. How many eggs will the family use in the month of March?

Which words in David's problem have hidden number ideas in them?

Rewrite the problem using numerals instead of the words which have a hidden number idea. This rewriting of a problem is a simple paraphrasing. You keep the original meaning of the problem, but you use numerals instead of words.

Here again you see the importance of knowing the meanings of the words used in arithmetic. These words are the ones which are used for units of measure—words like *dozen* and *month of March* in David's problem. Learn to RECOGNIZE IMPORTANT DETAILS such as these, and you will be more successful in arithmetic.

Words for units of measure will be used in the crossnumber puzzle which follows. You will need to know the tables for dry and liquid measure. Knowledge of the tables of measure for time, weight, money, length, area, and counting will also be necessary.

Make a copy of the crossnumber puzzle found on page 242. Work the crossnumber puzzle in the same way you work a crossword puzzle.

If you come to a unit of measure which you do not know and look for its meaning in another source, you will be demonstrating that you use two parts of an important reading rule: RECOGNIZE THE NEED FOR MORE INFORMATION and LOCATE INFORMATION OUTSIDE YOUR TEXT.

Across

a. 5 quarters = ____ cents
c. 3 weeks = ____ hours
e. In 2 miles there are ____ yards.
h. 6 pints = ____ cups
j. In 10 bushels there are ____ pecks.
k. 1 yard 2 feet 5 inches = ____ inches

l. 5 centuries and 1 decade = ____ years

n. In 7 weeks there are ____ days.

o. A dollar is worth ____ more cents than a dime.

p. ____ hours = 20 days

q. 4 ounces less than a pound = ____ ounces

r. ____ seconds = 1 minute 3 seconds

s. Four score and 7 years = ____ years.

u. 3141 feet more than a mile = ____ feet

w. 28 gallons = ____ pints

x. There are ____ pints in 5 bushels.

Down

a. A century and 1 year = ____ years.

b. 7 minutes less than 1 hour = ____ minutes

c. 10 gallons and 10 quarts = ____ quarts

d. ____ cents = 17 quarters

f. In 9 hours there are ____ minutes.

g. 1 and ½ days have ____ more hours than a pound has ounces.

i. 2 square yards = ____ square inches

k. ____ pounds = 908 pounds more than 3 tons

m. A minute has ____ more seconds than the number of cents in a half dollar.

n. 4 dozen eggs = ____ eggs

p. ____ square inches = 3 square feet

q. 7 gallons = ____ cups

r. In 4 pounds there are ____ ounces.

t. 2 common years = ____ days

u. 7 dozen eggs = ____ eggs

v. $2.60 = ____ scores of cents

UNDERSTANDING RELATIONSHIPS

How well have you learned to get basic number ideas from words? Test your ability to get these ideas in each of the following exercises. Give the number which results from establishing the relationship that is required. You will find that you will FIT YOUR SPEED TO YOUR NEEDS as you READ TO UNDERSTAND RELATIONSHIPS.

See how many of the exercises you can do mentally:

1. Half of 10
2. Twice 8
3. 7 less than 12
4. The sum of 5 and 6
5. 3 more than twice 9
6. 5 less than half of 23
7. The sum of 7 and half of 8
8. Half the sum of 36 and 4
9. Twice the sum of 3 and 11
10. The difference between 15 and 7
11. The difference between 18 and one-third of 12
12. The product of 9 and 8
13. Half of the product of 4 and 3
14. 3 less than the product of 5 and 7
15. 4 ounces more than half a pound
16. The sum of twice 7 and one-fourth of 8

17. 4 more than 9, plus 3 less
    than half of 20
18. 24 divided by twice 3
19. The number of inches in a foot
    less than one yard
20. The quotient when the product
    of 4 and 6 is divided by the sum
    of 3 and 5.

In the work you have just completed, you began with some easy exercises in seeing relationships. But before you were through, you were working on much more difficult relationships and were building your ability in this skill to a very high level.

The groups of exercises and word problems which follow will give you further practice in seeing number relationships. One exercise in each group will require you to do the same kind of thinking that you do in the word problem which follows. Work each group of exercises and problems.

Examine carefully the sequence of thinking you had to follow in order to work each problem. Watch for steps in the sequence which may seem insignificant! Then look for *one* of the exercises, which precede each problem, that requires an identical sequence of thinking. Match each problem with one exercise in each group. The example given after the first problem will provide you with a pattern to follow as you do the matching.

(a) Add 4 and 7. Then subtract the sum of 3 and 5.

(b) How many gallons are in a dozen quarts?

(c) Find 4 more than twice 9. Subtract half of 10.

(d) Find twice the sum of 22 and 8.

1. Anna bought six 8-cent stamps and a 5-cent stamp. How much more than a half dollar did she pay for the stamps? (_1_ matches _(c)_ because in both situations you first had to *multiply*, then *add*, then *find* ½ of something, and finally *subtract* in order to follow the directions given in the exercise and problem.)

1.
$$8 \times 6 = 48 \qquad 48 + 5 = 53 \qquad \tfrac{1}{2} \text{ of } 100 = 50 \qquad 53 - 50 = 3$$

(c)
$$9 \times 2 = 18 \qquad 18 + 4 = 22 \qquad \tfrac{1}{2} \text{ of } 10 = 5 \qquad 22 - 5 = 17$$

(a) If 7 more than a certain number is 19, what is the number?

(b) The sum of three numbers is 16. Two of the numbers are 3 and 7. Find the other number.

(c) Find the difference between 15 and 7. Multiply it by one-third of the product of 2 and 9.

(*d*) Add half of 14 to one-fourth of 8. Subtract 2 more than 3. If you use the result as one factor of 20, what is the other factor?

2. Don has a dollar to spend at the fair. He spends 30¢ for a ticket and 50¢ for food. How much does he still have to spend? (____ matches ____ because . . . .)

(*a*) What is 6 less than twice the product of 7 and 2?

(*b*) If a pound contains more than a score of ounces, tell the number of days in 5 weeks. If it doesn't, tell the number of minutes in 3 hours.

(*c*) Add 3 less than 7 to 5 more than 8. Subtract 1 and find half of the result. If this is an *even* number, tell the number of days in a common year. If not, tell the number of feet in a mile.

(*d*) Find the quotient if 8 more than 32 is divided by twice 5.

3. David worked from 2 o'clock till 5 o'clock delivering packages. If he was paid 80¢ an hour, how much did he earn? (____ matches ____ because . . . .)

(*a*) Twice 8 is how much more than one-third of 21?

(b) If there are more minutes in an hour than there are seconds in a minute, give the number of inches in 2 yards. If not, give the number of hours in 2 days.

(c) If the difference between two numbers is 11 and the smaller number is 14, what is the larger number?

(d) Take half of 8 and multiply it by 3. Subtract the product of 2 and 6.

4. Amy went to the store and bought two dozen oranges. There were 10 oranges left, and Amy's friend, Karla, bought half of them. How many more oranges were bought by Amy than by Karla? (____ matches ____ because . . . .)

(a) How many dozen inches are there in a yard? Subtract this number from the number of decades in a century.

(b) The difference between two numbers is 7, and the larger number is 13. Find the product of the smaller number and 10.

(c) Subtract 6 from half of 20. Add 4. Multiply the result by 5 and divide by 2.

(d) How much larger is the product of 3 and 6 than the difference between 20 and 32?

5. In a game, Charlotte scored 8 points on each of two different plays. Laura ran her score up to 24 points and then lost 10 points. Which girl won the game, and by how many points? (____ matches ____ because . . . .)

Check your answers with the list which follows:

   (*a*) 3   (*b*) 3   (*c*) 17   (*d*) 60

1. 3: *1* matches (*c*)

   (*a*) 12   (*b*) 6   (*c*) 48   (*d*) 5

2. 20: *2* matches (*b*)

   (*a*) 22   (*b*) 180   (*c*) 365   (*d*) 4

3. $2.40: *3* matches (*b*)

   (*a*) 9   (*b*) 48   (*c*) 25   (*d*) 0

4. 19: *4* matches (*a*)

   (*a*) 7   (*b*) 60   (*c*) 20   (*d*) 6

5. Charlotte—2: *5* matches (*d*)

If you have incorrect answers, reread the exercises or problems you missed. Analyze your errors. Did you misinterpret the directions given by the words, or were your errors caused by mistakes in addition, subtraction, multiplication, or division? If you had errors, correct them.

MEETING CHALLENGES TO YOUR WORD POWER

You are now going to test your ability to use your word power through meeting some special challenges. CONCENTRATE and KNOW WHAT YOU READ, and you will be able to meet these challenges to your word power.

Challenge 1: Can you handle twists and turns in directions? Try this rambling recipe for making a strange mixture:

Take the number of inches in a foot and add the number of quarts in a gallon. Subtract the number of days in a week. Multiply by the number of feet in a yard. Subtract the number of pints in a quart. Divide by the number of cents in a nickel. If you had this many eggs, how many more would you need to make a dozen?

Challenge 2: Can you follow the directions that words give you? The ability to follow directions is of great importance in arithmetic. The work that comes next will help you to test this ability in yourself.

Use this list of number symbols and answer the questions which follow:

24   17   10   31   28   7   15

a. What is the largest number? the largest *even* number?

b. What is the smallest number? the smallest *odd* number?

c. What is the difference between the largest *odd* number and the smallest *even* number?

d. What is the sum of all the *odd* numbers if the second largest odd number is left out?

e. What is the product of the numbers that are larger than 11 but smaller than 22?

f. What is the quotient when the divisor is 3 less than the smallest number and the dividend is 6 more than half the largest *even* number?

Challenge 3: Can you find and handle the number relationships that words describe? You will have to read and reason carefully to do the following work.

The four children in the Rogers family earn money by working in their father's store. Jack has earned $4, and Linda has earned $3 more than Jack. Mary has earned $2 more than Linda. And Fred has earned $4 less than the sum of the earnings of Linda and Mary.

a. How much has been earned by Jack? by Linda? by Mary? by Fred?

b. The child with the largest earnings has how much more than the child with the smallest earnings?

c. How much has been earned by all the Rogers children?

d. If Fred gave Jack $3, which children would have the same amount?

e. If all the money earned were divided equally among the four children, how much more would Linda have than she has now?

Challenge 4: Can you use words as guides when

251

you work with sets of things? Application of the reading rules will be very important here.

In one class, 7 students belong to the Drama Club and 10 students belong to the Music Club. Members of the Drama Club can also be members of the Music Club if they wish.

a. How many students are members of at least one club if no students are members of both clubs? if just 2 students are members of both clubs? if 5 students are members of both clubs?

b. What is the smallest number of students who could be members of at least one club and still have 7 students in the Drama Club and 10 students in the Music Club?

Now refer to the reading rules on page 13. Tell which rules you applied as you worked each challenge. Why did you apply these rules?

USING ARITHMETIC WORDS
IN OTHER WAYS

Many arithmetic words are used when you talk or write about everyday happenings. As you read the following sentences, think about the meaning of each underlined word. Then tell how the arithmetical meaning of each word is related to the meaning the word has in the sentence.

1. "Alice will <u>sum</u> up the report of the Science Club's work," said the teacher.

2. The rain was one <u>factor</u> in changing our plans for a picnic.

3. I've <u>half</u> decided to vote for Jim.

4. Many departments coöperated to create this <u>product</u>.

5. For the <u>remainder</u> of the class hour we will read stories.

6. Traffic was so heavy that our car could only <u>inch</u> along the highway.

7. He's always in a <u>peck</u> of trouble.

8. <u>Dividing</u> the work made everyone's task easier.

9. The <u>pint</u>-sized blanket didn't begin to cover Big Joe.

10. What a <u>difference</u> it makes to get rid of that heavy overcoat!

11. "An <u>ounce</u> of prevention is worth a <u>pound</u> of cure," is one of Benjamin Franklin's sayings.

12. Excitement <u>multiplied</u> as the team fought hard to win the game.

Find three sentences in newspapers, or magazines, or other books, in which words you have met in arithmetic are being used in ways that do not involve number work. Or try to write three such sentences of your own. Tell how each word's meaning in arithmetic is related to its meaning in the sentence.

KNOWING WORD HISTORY

In arithmetic, as in other subjects, finding the meaning of one valuable word may give you the clue to the meanings of a whole set of words.

Suppose you discover that the word *meter* comes from the Greek *metron* which means "measure." Use this meaning clue and add *meter* to the unfinished words which follow. Next tell the meaning of as many of the words as you can. That is, tell what is being measured in each case. Then use the Glossary for any word you did not know.

1. Thermo-----	5. Alti-----
2. Speedo-----	6. Chrono-----
3. Peri-----	7. Calori-----
4. Dia-----	8. Volt-----

Now do some work on word history yourself. *Multi* comes from Latin and means "many." *Tri* comes from Latin and means "three."

Use your dictionary and find at least three words that begin with "multi" and have the idea of *many* in their meaning. Use the words you have selected in sentences of your own.

Find at least three words that begin with "tri." Be sure that each one has the idea of *three* in its meaning. Use these words in sentences.

The words which follow have number ideas *hidden* in them. Tell the meaning of and the hidden number

idea in as many words as you can. Use the Glossary
to find the meaning and pronunciation of any words
which you do not know.

1. Hemisphere
2. Pentagon
3. Quintuplets
4. Sextet

5. Octopus
6. Decimal
7. Centennial
8. Per cent

Use each of the preceding words in a sentence to
prove that you know the hidden number idea. Which
of the following sentences proves that the writer
knew the hidden number idea in the word *octopus?*

1. The sight of the eight waving arms of the
octopus was frightening.
2. The octopus was a frightening sight.

List as many other words as you can which have
a number idea hidden in them. Combine all the words
from the lists of your classmates. Of course you
will not list a word twice. Discuss the meaning of
each word in the class list. Use these words in sentences to prove that you know the number idea
hidden in each word.

READING HUGE-NUMBER WORDS

People living and working in the space age have
to deal with huge-number ideas. It is not unusual

to read the words "million," "billion," and "trillion" in newspapers, magazines, and books. It is difficult, however, for the average person to imagine how large a million or even a thousand of something is.

One way for you to develop a better understanding of the symbols which represent huge-number ideas is to BUILD MENTAL IMAGES. To build a mental image you will need to see the amount represented by one number symbol. Then compare this idea with a symbol representing a larger amount. Finally, try to imagine the size of a huge-number idea.

The illustration on the next page pictures 1,000 stars. If you use the same illustration, how many pages of this size will be needed to picture 3,000 stars? The concept of 3,000 stars on three pages is not a difficult one.

A million is a thousand thousands. How many pages will be needed to illustrate a million stars? How many pages are there in this book? Can you see that it would take about three books of this size to illustrate a million stars?

A billion is a thousand millions. How many books would it take to illustrate a billion stars? Now you are dealing with a really huge-number idea.

Some other words which represent huge-number ideas are:

1. A trillion is a thousand billions.
2. A quadrillion is a thousand trillions.

257

3. A quintillion is a thousand quadrillions.

If you wrote "one quintillion," it would look like this:

1,000,000,000,000,000,000

It is much easier to read the words "one quintillion" than to read the numerals which represent this huge-number idea. For this reason, many writers use a combination of words and numerals when they wish to indicate huge-number ideas.

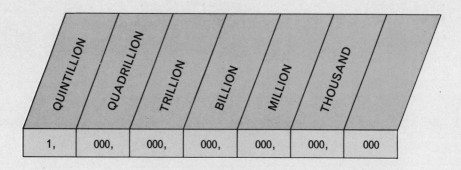

QUINTILLION	QUADRILLION	TRILLION	BILLION	MILLION	THOUSAND	
1,	000,	000,	000,	000,	000,	000

The next six statements have been taken from recent newspaper and magazine articles. Read the statements. Then see if you can translate the word and numeral combination used by the writers into a numeral which represents the huge-number idea. The chart will help you write the large numerals. Be sure to place a comma between each "period" of three digits, counting from right to left. Of course when you *read* the huge number, read from left to right as usual. The first statement has been translated for you.

1. In a day the earth rotates on its axis and revolves around the sun at the same time. In one day a spot on the earth travels more than 1½ million miles. [*Translation:* 1,500,000 miles]

2. Gagarin's space ship traveled 17,000 miles per hour. In the future, space stations may be established which will be in orbit for weeks, months, and even years. If a space station traveled at 17,000 miles an hour for 10 years, it would travel about 3 billion miles.

3. There are at least 100 billion stars in our Milky Way Galaxy.

4. Astronomers use the light-year as a unit of measure when they speak or write about astronomical distances. Light travels 6 trillion miles in one light-year.

5. Antares, one of the brightest stars which can be seen in the heavens, is more than 2 quadrillion miles away from the earth.

6. The distance across the Milky Way is about 6 quintillion miles.

Here is an old fable which is based on a huge-number idea:

Many, many years ago a prince wanted to reward the man who had invented the game of chess.

"What reward can I give you?" asked the prince.

"Sire," answered the man, with a twinkle in his eye, "I do not ask for much. Just give me one grain of wheat for the first square on the chessboard, two grains for the second square, and four grains for the third square. Double four grains for the fourth square and continue doubling the grains of wheat for each successive square."

"Your request shall be granted at once," said the prince, who hadn't studied very much arithmetic.

Do you have any idea of how many grains of wheat it would take to pay this reward? There are several ways to figure this problem. One way would be to make a table like this:

Square	Grains	Total Grains
1	1	⌐ 1
2	2	1 + 2 = 3
3	4	3 + 4 = 7
4	8	7 + 8 = 15
5	16	15 + 16 = 31
etc.	etc.	etc.
64	etc.	etc.

If you continue this table you will find that the total number of grains of wheat promised was 18,466,744,073,709,551,615.

A mathematician has figured that this number of wheat grains would equal over 28 trillion bushels of wheat. This is more wheat than the United States could produce in 22,000 years!

Why do you think the man who made the request had a twinkle in his eye?

INTERPRETING THE REMAINDER

It is easy to record the remainder when you are doing drill examples in division. You probably record the remainder like one of these:

$$
\begin{array}{r}
85 \\
6)\overline{513} \\
48 \\
\hline
33 \\
30 \\
\hline
3 \text{ left over}
\end{array}
\quad \text{or} \quad
\begin{array}{r}
85 \text{ r}3 \\
6)\overline{513} \\
48 \\
\hline
33 \\
30 \\
\hline
3
\end{array}
\quad \text{or} \quad
\begin{array}{r}
85\frac{3}{6} = 85\frac{1}{2} \\
6)\overline{513} \\
48 \\
\hline
33 \\
30 \\
\hline
\cancel{3}
\end{array}
$$

But in story problems dealing with division, your interpretation of what the remainder means will affect the way you record your answer. You will need to use your reading and thinking skills to—

a. Analyze the question asked.

b. Interpret the remainder.

c. Discover what the remainder means.

d. See how the remainder affects the quotient.

Work the following division problems mentally. Read the instruction in the box which precedes each problem. Think about the details in each problem and the hidden meaning in the situation. Tell why the remainder is interpreted as it is, and tell whether or not it affects the quotient.

A. Think of the remainder as something left over and not a part of the quotient. Why?

Four boys have $.50 to share equally. What is the largest amount each boy can have?

B. Increase the quotient by one in this problem. Why?

Eight students can eat at one table in the cafeteria. How many tables are needed when 175 students eat at one time?

C. Express the remainder as a fraction and consider it a part of the quotient in this problem. Why?

Three girls have four small pies to share equally. What is each girl's share?

D. Drop the remainder in this problem. Why?

A strip of cardboard is 30 inches long. How many 4-inch bookmarks can be cut from the strip?

Now test your ability to interpret the *remainder* in the following problems. What question is asked in each problem? What is the relationship between the remainder and the quotient? Work each problem and then tell how you interpreted the remainder and how it affected the quotient.

1. The students at Hughes School have chosen blue for their school color. They want to make badges to wear to the next ball game. How many 5-inch badges can they make from 47 yards of ribbon?

2. Mr. Dickinson has been asked to move 542 chairs to the gymnasium. If he has a cart which will carry 24 chairs, how many trips must he make?

3. Twenty-seven boys in Elk Rapids decided to collect old magazines and newspapers. They sold them for $10.24. What was each boy's share of the money?

4. In a company test of gasoline mileage, a car's gasoline tank was filled with 18 gallons of gasoline. The test car traveled 654 miles before it ran out of gas. What mileage record per gallon did the company report?

5. Fifteen bicycles can be placed in one bicycle rack at Liberty School. If 127 students own bicycles and ride them to school each day, how many racks are needed?

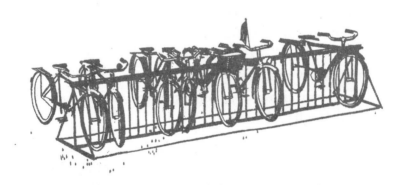

In the five preceding problems you had to know more than the meaning of the words. You had to think about the situation which the words described. Actually, you used common sense in order to draw your conclusions and interpret the remainders. You were thinking carefully as you read.

UNIT SIX

Reading Science

ORGANIZING WHAT YOU READ

The first step in organizing what you have read is to recognize the order, or sequence, in which things happen.

As you read science, you will KNOW WHAT YOU READ and remember it longer if you organize your information into an outline. An outline also serves as a reminder when you are making a report.

Read the following paragraph on "The Scientific Method" and look for the five main steps in this method. Use "The Scientific Method" as a title for your outline. List the five steps in correct sequence as five main heads. If you have forgotten the form of an outline, use the index of your English textbook to help you locate a sample outline quickly.

The Scientific Method

The scientist goes about his work in a special way known as the *scientific method*. In a way it is a misunderstood term, because many people think that only scientists need to work this way. Actually, the scientific method applies in business and industry, home workshops, and schoolrooms just as much as it does in a science laboratory. Any other way of working on a problem may end up with incomplete or wrong results.

A scientist works in an orderly way and expects other scientists to work in the same way. Results will not be accepted unless the work is done this way. When you have finished this section, ask yourself if you shouldn't work in this way too.

Steps in the scientific method. To make discoveries, the scientist first states his problem. He states it either mentally or on paper. He knows the problem to state because he is in a situation where a problem exists. He is sensitive to things that need doing.

He then gathers all the information he can about his problem. What is already known? What, if any, prior attempts have been made to solve this problem? If there have been failures, how can he avoid committing these same errors again?

From this information, he makes a guess or a suggestion which he thinks will explain his problem. This guess is called an *hypothesis*. Of course, his hypothesis must be one which can be tested.

The next step is to devise an experiment or experiments which he thinks will test his hypothesis. He performs the experiments carefully and observes them closely. He keeps careful records of his observations. He repeats the experiments and sometimes he asks someone else to repeat the experiment.

In time the scientist is ready to judge the results of his experimentation. He decides whether his hypothesis was right or wrong; he draws a conclusion.

If his conclusion is that his hypothesis was wrong, he will often make another guess and start all over again. Edison tested hundreds of substances before he found something he could use to make a filament in his first electric light bulb. Someone sympathized with him, saying how discouraging it must have been to have suffered all those failures. Edison is supposed to have replied that he had no failures; each test had proved that something wouldn't work.

Does your outline resemble this outline? The words do not have to be exactly the same, but they should express the same idea.

The Scientific Method
  I. State a problem
 II. Gather information
III. Form an hypothesis

IV. Experiment and record
V. Draw conclusion from results

TAKING NOTES TO HELP YOU REMEMBER

As you read the following story, "A Scientist
Makes a Discovery," take notes as you find the
answers to these questions:
  1. What was the scientist's problem?
  2. What information did he already have?
  3. What was his hypothesis?
  4. What experiment did he perform?
  5. What conclusions did he draw?

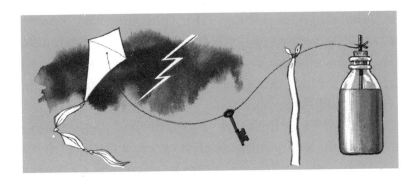

A Scientist Makes a Discovery

Benjamin Franklin once conducted a scientific experiment for which he earned much renown. That
was in 1752, and by that time something was known
about electricity, although it wasn't much more than

a laboratory plaything. But nothing was known about the nature of lightning. No one had been able to say what lightning is. Franklin had speculated that lightning and electricity were the same thing. How could he prove this?

Like all experimenters, Franklin had some reason for stating an hypothesis. His work with electricity and his observations of lightning gave him a number of clues that led him to say, "I think that lightning is an electrical charge." Having stated such an idea, the next thing he had to do was to find out whether his hypothesis was right or wrong. To do that, he devised an experiment. He decided that if he could bring lightning down out of the sky, he could test

whether or not it was electricity. Then he would have facts which he hoped would prove his hypothesis.

So he built a kite from a big silk handkerchief and put a metal point in the middle of the kite. He already knew from other experiments that such a metal point would make a kind of target for lightning. He used an ordinary kite string and tied an iron door key to the end. He had no intention of holding on to the string! The second thing he already knew was that if lightning were indeed electricity it would run down a wet kite string and into his body and electrocute him. So he tied a piece of silk to the string. Why did he use silk? Earlier work had taught him that silk was a poor conductor of electricity.

Now he was ready, and in a few days a violent storm broke out. Franklin let the wind lift his kite skyward. Soon, as he had expected, lightning struck the metal point. Instantly the electrical charge traveled down the wet kite string. He touched the iron door key and felt a shock. Yes, that was electricity, as he knew perfectly well. How often he and his friends had felt that same thing from their laboratory apparatus!

Franklin knew that the experiment was not yet over. He had to do more. After all, a feeling in a man's hand is not the kind of proof that other scientists would accept. He had at his side a device called a Leyden jar, in which electricity can be stored. Quickly Franklin touched the key to the Leyden jar, and electricity flowed from the kite into the jar. Now he had corroborating proof for his hypothesis. He had shown in two ways that lightning is a charge of electricity. Now no one could doubt the truth of his hypothesis!

After you have discussed the answers to the questions on page 269, one member of the class may give a report on "A Scientist Makes a Discovery." The reporter can use for a guide the outline which starts on page 268.

Since all class members have read the article, they will be listening carefully for details which may have been omitted or for information which may have been incorrectly reported. A discussion of the report will be helpful to the listeners as well as to the reporter. In this way, all class members will have an opportunity to check the effectiveness of their reading.

USING SIDEHEADS TO PREVIEW

The following article, titled "Sand to Glass to Lenses," is divided into several parts. You can recognize the parts because they are indicated by SIDEHEADS printed in heavy letters. Your PURPOSE for previewing this article is to learn to use *sideheads* more effectively. Preview the article from page 274 through page 281 and read the sideheads. The sideheads will give you an idea of the contents of the article before you start to read.

List the sideheads on a piece of paper or on the chalkboard. Without referring to the article, see if you can tell which sideheads contain information to prove the accuracy of these statements.

1. Some lenses are shaped so that they bulge outward.

2. Some scientific tools are simple and some are complicated.

3. When light rays move through a lens, they bend. This bending is called *refraction*.

4. Sand, potash, and lime when subjected to extreme heat blend to make glass.

5. Crude microscopes were in use more than 300 years ago.

6. Glass of excellent quality is needed to make lenses.

Now read the article carefully to see if you selected the correct sidehead to prove the accuracy of the six statements. You will need to FIT YOUR SPEED TO YOUR NEEDS, KNOW THE MEANING OF EVERY WORD, and CONCENTRATE ON DETAILS.

Sand to Glass to Lenses

The scientist's tools. The tools a scientist uses are determined by the experiment he wishes to perform. Some of these tools are exceedingly simple. Franklin used such tools as a kite, a metal point, and a handkerchief to prove his hypothesis about the nature of lightning. Other scientific tools are infinitely more complicated. A scientist might need a tool so sensitive that it could weigh the amount of material in a pencil dot. Another scientist might need presses so powerful that they could twist and mash steel beams as if they were made of straw.

Many of the tools a scientist utilizes are familiar to everyone. The thermometer and scales are found in many homes as well as in laboratories. Other scientific tools, such as the test tube and the Leyden jar, are found chiefly in the laboratory.

On the following pages you will read about three important scientific tools—the microscope, the telescope, and the camera. Without the microscope we would know very little about the world of tiny things. The telescope has permitted man to extend his knowledge to the unimaginable limits of space. The camera makes a permanent record.

The importance of sand. Each of these tools usually depends on one very important thing—*sand*. The proper process of combining sand, soda or potash, and lime under intense heat will produce glass.

Fused silica, a new type of glass for big telescope lenses, is inspected before being ground and polished.

Glass and sometimes plastic or quartz are used to make lenses. Glass is cheap; it is durable; it is non-porous. Some glass is transparent, which means that you can see through it.

No one knows for sure when or where the first glass was made. Pliny the Elder suggested that sailors who built a fire in the sand on a seacoast found chunks of glass after the fire died down. But modern research has traced glass to a much earlier date. Archeologists have found glass in Egypt that may have been there more than 5,000 years. There are records to prove that the countries of the early Roman Empire manufactured glass. Forces of nature may have made glass too. Observers believe that certain glass-like objects which they have found near a volcano may have been formed because of its intense heat. Isn't it amazing that such a common thing as sand is used to produce such a vital product as glass?

Glass used for lenses. The sand used to produce glass for lenses must be carefully selected. Sand grains of an even size and without dust are chosen. After the glass is produced it must be properly shaped and ground to a smooth and even finish. The glass for lenses must be of high quality and the workmanship perfect. Glass lenses make it possible for men to see things which the eye cannot see unaided. Lenses make the invisible *visible*. Microscopes, telescopes, and cameras need lenses to help the scientist do his work.

Shapes of lenses. The shape of the lens determines its use. There are two main shapes of lenses, concave and convex. The convex lens bulges outward and the concave lens curves inward. The convex lens causes light rays to converge, or come together. The concave lens causes the rays to diverge. Sometimes the lenses are used in pairs as double lenses. The double concave lens is made up of two lenses curved inward. The double convex lens is made up of two lenses curved outward.

Light and lenses. In order to understand how a lens works, we must first know about light. As everyone knows, we cannot see without light. Light comes from an object and brings sight to our eyes. Nothing goes from our eyes to the object. Few objects give off light of their own, but light from the sun is reflected from things all around us. Light also comes from an artificial source such as a lamp. You can see your pencil because it is reflecting light from one of these sources, and an image of the pencil is transmitted to your eyes.

Light reaches our eyes in rays or straight lines. These rays always move along the same straight line within the same material. But as a light ray passes from one transparent material to another, it bends. Light bends, for example, when it moves from air into water. We call this bending *refraction*.

You can perform an experiment to observe refraction. Place a pencil in a glass of water. Does the pencil seem to bend at the surface of the water? This "bending" is caused by refraction. Remove the pencil. Is it bent? Of course not, it just looked bent. The light rays from the pencil angled off in another direction as they moved into the water from the air. The angling light rays created the false image of the pencil bending.

A light ray also bends as it moves through a lens or lenses. It is this bending which permits us to see such tiny things as bacteria and things which are large but are 3 quadrillion miles away.

Early inventions and later applications. Sometimes people think that things very useful to them must be modern or contemporary inventions. That is not necessarily true. Much of modern mathematics has been known for centuries. Principles of architecture have changed because of newer materials, such as steel and reinforced concrete. But the Romans used concrete 2,000 years ago. Microscopes and telescopes have been in use for hundreds of years. It is said that a simple pinhole camera was in use before the birth of Christ.

A Dutch instrument maker, Anton van Leeuwenhoek, began to use microscopes as a research tool about 300 years ago. Crude microscopes had been in existence for some time, but no one had put them to their best use. Biographers now refer to Leeuwenhoek as a microscopist—a specialist in the use of microscopes. He manufactured microscopes for himself and for others. He ground his lenses accurately and he worked carefully. He examined and described almost everything he laid his hands on: the eyes of insects, the eggs of ants, the petals of flowers. He peered closely at blood samples and gave us the first accurate description of blood cells. One sketch shows that he examined what scientists have now identified as bacteria.

Today a whole branch of science, bacteriology, is devoted to the study of bacteria. In this study, the microscope is relied upon greatly to assist the scientist in his examination of all kinds of both harmful and helpful bacteria.

An Italian, Galileo, one of the greatest men of science, was the first to explore space with a telescope. He had heard that a Dutchman was working with lenses. Once, accidentally, the Dutchman's

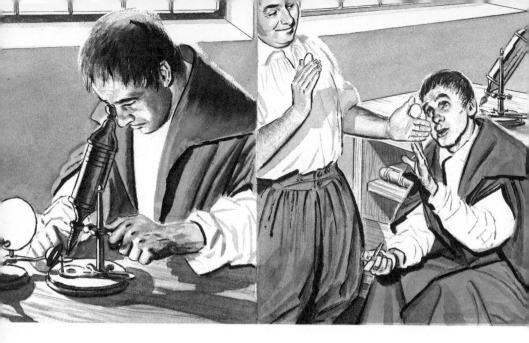

assistant held two lenses a foot or two apart. Looking through both lenses at once, the assistant observed an astounding thing—objects brought into view were magnified. When Galileo heard of this experience, he used two lenses and made a telescope for himself.

Soon Galileo made many important discoveries in astronomy. One night he looked closely at the planet Jupiter through his telescope. At first he could see only two nearby stars. On a later night he spotted four stars and noticed that the stars were not always in the same place. They moved around. Suddenly he understood. The "stars" were not stars after all. They were moons!

Astronomers have now discovered twelve moons of Jupiter. The telescope is enabling astronomers to pursue their study and make new discoveries.

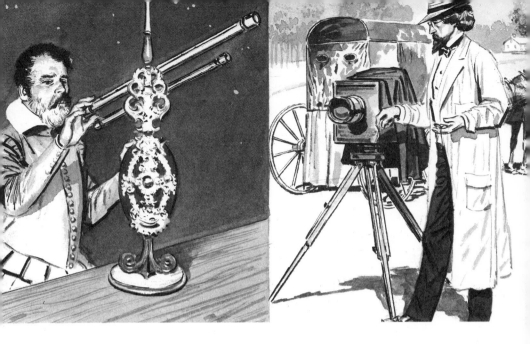

The camera has been a useful tool for more than a hundred years. Mathew Brady and his team of photographers made thousands of excellent photographs of the War between the States. But before this he had become well known for his portrait photographs of important men and women. Brady's photographs have given us an accurate record of the people and events of his time. In those days, and for a long time afterwards, photography was quite difficult and was undertaken only by experts.

Today a scientist who wishes to study the blast-off of a rocket has only an instant to observe it. With a camera a series of photographs can be taken of the blast-off. These photographs give him a permanent record. He can study and restudy the performance of the rocket during the instant of blast-off.

"Sand to Glass to Lenses" has provided you with a background of information which will make the remainder of this Unit more meaningful. To be certain that you know this information, try to answer the following questions without rereading the article. If you find questions you cannot answer, you will need to reread. Be economical in your use of time. Use your sideheads for more efficient rereading.

Read orally the part or parts of the section which prove that your answers are correct.

1. What is one modern use of the microscope? the telescope? the camera?
2. How is a concave lens different from a convex lens?
3. What is refraction?
4. What was the relationship between the invention of the microscope and the telescope?
5. Why do different scientists use different tools?
6. What happens to light rays when they pass through a convex lens?
7. What is the relationship between sand and scientific discoveries?

RECOGNIZING WHEN TO USE CONTEXT CLUES

Some of the words in the list which follows are defined in the paragraph where they occur. Some of the words are not defined. A good reader watches for and uses context clues. He also must recognize when he needs to turn to the Glossary or use a dictionary for word meanings. Test your skill in determining whether to use context clues, Glossary, or dictionary to learn meanings of words.

Give the definitions of as many of the following words as you can. Then turn to the pages indicated and tell which words were defined in the context. What was the context clue for each word? The words for which there is no context clue will need to be checked for meaning in your Glossary.

Page 267, sensitive

Page 276, transparent

Page 267, hypothesis

Page 277, converge

Page 267, devise

Page 277, diverge

Page 268, filament

Page 278, angled

Page 272, apparatus

Page 278, contemporary

Page 272, Leyden jar

Page 279, microscopist

Page 273, refraction

Page 279, bacteriology

Page 275, permanent

Page 281, portrait

As you continue to read this book and other books, watch for context clues which will define words for you. On the other hand, if the word is not defined in context, be sure to use the Glossary or dictionary.

TAKING NOTES AS YOU READ

When the scientist performs an experiment, he pursues his work in a systematic way. He is careful to take each step in the right sequence and he makes accurate records of the result of his experiment. You as a reader need to work in this same systematic way.

Before you read "The Microscopic World," preview it by reading the sideheads. Copy these sideheads on a piece of paper. Leave five or six lines between each sidehead. Use these sideheads as a framework to follow and take notes as you read. Be sure your notes include the important details you find under each sidehead.

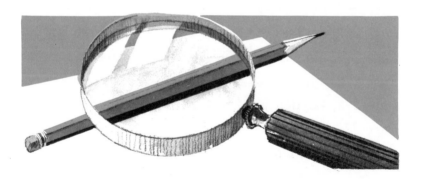

The Microscopic World

A magnifying glass. Scientists use lenses as aids to human eyes. The lenses are inserted into all sorts of holders or machines, depending on what each lens is to do.

A magnifying glass is a simple microscope. With a magnifying glass you can see the pore openings along the skin ridges on your finger. Or you can look at a color picture in a magazine or a book and see that it is made up of very small dots of color. Deprived of the magnifying glass, your eye sees an unbroken pattern of color and not a swarm of dots.

You can make a simple magnifying glass from a piece of wire, some vegetable oil, and a drop of water. Twist one end of the wire into a small loop. Coat the loop with vegetable oil. Now dip the loop into a glass of water, allowing a film of water to form across the loop. Lift the water-filled loop slowly from the glass. Hold the water-filled loop over a word in this book. See how the type is magnified! The film of water served as a lens in your simple magnifying glass.

Suppose you want to see something that a magnifying glass is not strong enough to show you. You need a microscope.

Uses of microscopes. Microscopes are used by physicians and surgeons in hospitals and clinics, by workers in manufacturing plants, by students in classrooms, and by research scientists in laboratories. With microscopes they can observe and study plant and animal life, blood cells, and other things too small for us to imagine.

Swarms of tiny animals called *protozoa* come to life in a drop of pond water. A drop of blood contains millions of red blood cells. These microscopic objects can be seen easily through a microscope.

Without the microscope, many other living and nonliving things would be lost to view. Suppose that you were to look at a butterfly wing through a microscope. You have seen the wing and have a good idea what it looks like. But beneath the microscope, the wing takes on new beauty. It is seen to be a delicate web with neat rows of overlapping scales exactly like

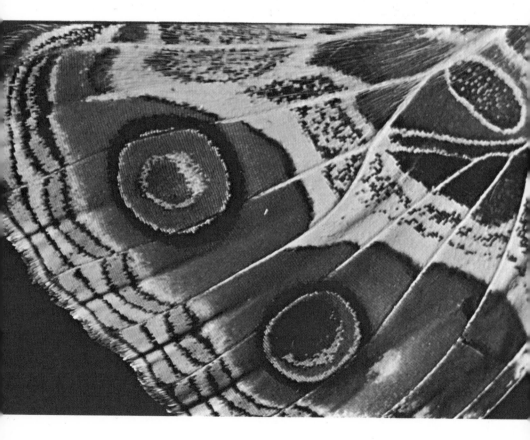

shingles on a roof. It is these scales that come off on your fingers and seem to be dust, when you handle a butterfly.

One use of the microscope that perhaps you would not think of is in water-purification plants. Technicians keep a constant check on what organisms are in the water so that they can know how much chlorine will be needed to purify the water.

Knowledge gained by the use of the microscope affects our lives in many ways. It has helped man conquer some diseases. It has helped biologists study

cell life. It has helped scientists study the structure of materials such as metals, plants, foods, drugs, cloth, paper, and many others. The microscope will continue to help man in his search for more knowledge.

The parts of a microscope. It is interesting to look through a microscope to see the world of things too small for the eye to see alone. It is also interesting to look at the microscope itself to find out how it functions.

A microscope could be described as a series of magnifying glasses. The lens is the most important part of a microscope. A laboratory microscope has several lenses. Such a microscope is called a compound microscope and is a more complicated device than an ordinary magnifying glass.

A microscope is made up of several parts. Each part has a name and a purpose. The base is the pedestal on which the instrument rests. Close to the base is a mirror. The mirror reflects light onto the object being viewed. Above the mirror is the stage. A slide (piece of glass) is placed on the stage. The object to be viewed is mounted on the slide.

The upper part of a microscope consists of a stand and two tubes. The stand holds the tubes in place. The upper tube fits snugly into the lower tube. The scientist adjusts the lenses to his eyes by turning knobs called "adjusting wheels." The adjusting wheels cause the upper tube to move up or down within the lower tube.

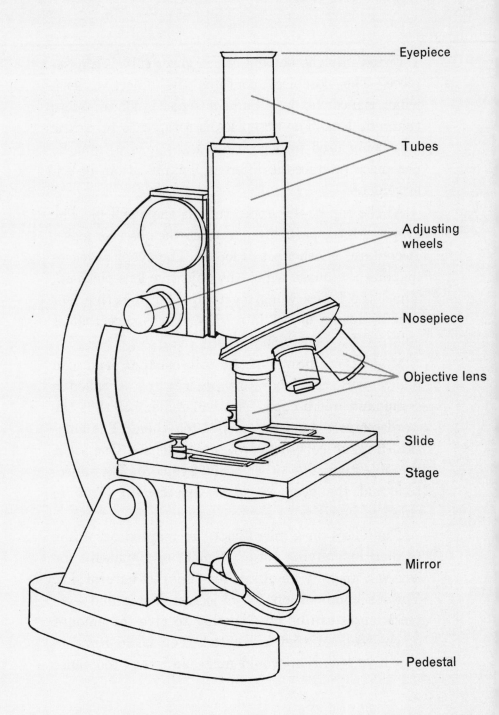

Eyepiece

Tubes

Adjusting
wheels

Nosepiece

Objective lens

Slide

Stage

Mirror

Pedestal

Fitted into the bottom of the lower tube is a nose-piece. The nosepiece contains the objective lens, which is a convex lens. Some nosepieces contain more than one lens. The nosepiece is rotated to bring the lens being used into position. Each lens within the nosepiece produces a different magnification, or enlargement.

At the top of the upper tube is the eyepiece. The eyepiece is the part through which the observer looks. It contains another set of lenses. The eyepiece lenses magnify the image which the objective lens picks up. Thus, the lenses work together. The objective lens first brings an object into view. This image then is enlarged by the eyepiece lens.

Magnifying power of the microscope. You can realize why the laboratory microscope is called a compound microscope. You will remember that the word *compound* means "to put together." The laboratory microscope uses two sets of lenses. One set is the objective. The other is the eyepiece. The objective and the eyepiece work together to form an enlarged image.

The lenses on a microscope are marked according to their magnifying power. A mark of 10x means the lens will magnify an object ten times its natural size. Various combinations of objective lenses and eyepiece lenses can be put together to give the amount of enlargement that is wanted. You could have an objective lens that would make an image ten times

Preparing a glass slide

as big as the thing being observed. Then you could have an eyepiece lens that would make that image ten times bigger. Multiply the power of the eyepiece by the power of the objective: 10 times 10 equals 100. What your eye sees is 100 times the actual size of the object. If you had a 30x objective lens with a 20x eyepiece, how much magnification would you have?

You might think that the bigger the magnification, the better. Not always. The greater the magnification the less of your specimen you see. Also, the amount of light reaching your eye is lessened. And with the greater magnification you can see clearly and sharply much *less* deeply into your specimen than you could see with the lower magnification.

Seeing the structure of an object. You can lay something—a leaf, a stone, an insect wing—on the stage of a microscope, beam light down on it, and look at it. What you will see is an enlarged view of the surface of the object. But more often what you want to see is the structure, and to do that you have to see below the surface.

To see below the surface the scientist cuts a slice of the specimen so thin that light can pass through it. How thin are those slices? Thinness varies a lot, depending on what is needed and what is possible. But the slices are commonly a half or a third of a thousandth of an inch thick. To get an idea of what a half of a thousandth of an inch is, a human hair is *two or three thousandths* of an inch in diameter.

Slices of such marvelous thinness are made in a machine called a microtome. Even a rock sliced on a microtome will usually permit the passage of light.

There is a great deal more to know about microscopy. Specimens are artificially colored in many ways to show their structure and nature. Specimens are prepared chemically in many ways before they are sliced. Many kinds of light can be brought to bear on the object being studied in the microscope.

Modern improvements in lenses. Since Anton van Leeuwenhoek's time, many improvements have been made in the construction of lenses. Glass is better and more uniform. Glass intended for use in instruments is made from a radically different formula from the formula used for glass intended for windows. We now have superior methods of grinding and polishing lenses. One great improvement has been made in resolving power of lenses. Resolving power is a characteristic of a lens, along with light-gathering and light-bending. Resolving power refers to the ability of a lens to let the viewer see that very small details or very distant details are indeed separate things.

The electron microscope. Even the finest of lens microscopes cannot magnify beyond a certain point. The nature of light itself puts a limit to the power of the lenses. When scientists need to study objects which cannot be seen by the ordinary microscope, they use the electron microscope.

The electron microscope uses electrons instead of light rays to form an image. Electrons are tiny particles that help to make up all forms of matter. They have a negative electrical charge and move in waves, just as light moves in waves. The electron microscope uses neither mirror nor lenses. It uses an electron gun, which is a device which can free electrons from a metal plate. The electron gun is the mirror of this microscope. Instead of lenses the electron microscope uses electromagnets.

When a scientist uses an electron microscope, he mounts the object to be viewed on a slide. The slide is only about two millionths of an inch thick. If the slide were any thicker, the electrons could not pass through it.

With the slide in place, the scientist turns on the electron microscope. Instantly the "gun" shoots a beam of electrons. The beam of electrons penetrates the specimen and slide, and forms a pattern which is an image of the specimen. But the image is invisible to the unaided eye! The beam then enters a magnetic field which was created by the electromagnets. The beams are collected and bent just as a lens refracts light. Or, to put it another way, the magnets spread the beam out or diffuse and magnify it.

To the human eye both the electron and the electron beam are invisible. To bring the image into view, the beam strikes a fluorescent screen within the microscope. As the electrons hit it, the screen emits light rays. Now the scientist can see the image on the screen. The image is much like a television picture. Sometimes the image is placed on a photographic plate instead of a screen.

The most powerful optical microscope enlarges an object 2,500 times. But the electron microscope can magnify an object 25,000 times its diameter. An electron-microscope photograph can be blown up even more. From these photographs an object can be magnified about 100,000 times.

The electron microscope has helped scientists learn about many things. One thing they are so anxious to

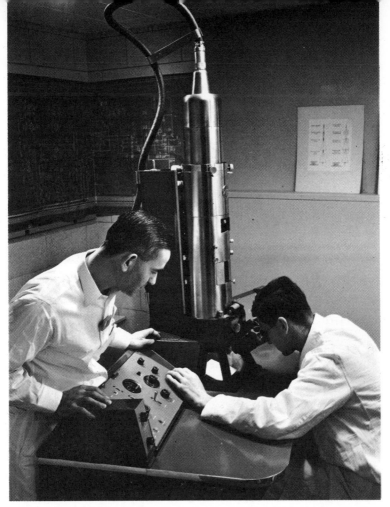

An electron microscope

learn more about is the virus. Viruses, if alive, are
the smallest living things. They cause such diseases
as measles and poliomyelitis. Scientists know about
the make-up of a virus and what it does. But there is
much they do not know. Someday scientists will solve
the riddle of the virus. The electron microscope will
help them.

How successful were you in recognizing important details and in taking notes? Without referring to your book, discuss one of the eight following statements. When you have finished your discussion, your classmates will add any important details which you might have omitted. If you disagree on the details, compare your notes with the information given in your text. All class members have an obligation to listen carefully and to check the accuracy of their reading. Continue in this way until the remaining seven statements have been discussed by different students.

1. Simple microscopes such as the magnifying glass can be used when you do not wish a great magnification of the object.

2. Electron microscopes do not depend upon lenses and mirrors in the same way an ordinary microscope does.

3. Knowledge gained by the use of microscopes has affected our lives in many ways.

4. The power of the objective lens and the power of the eyepiece lens of a microscope are combined to form an enlarged image.

5. A microscope is made up of several parts. (You may use the diagram on page 289 to help you.)

6. When you want to look at the structure of an object rather than its surface, you must use a very thin slice of the object.

7. Microscopes are used by many people doing different kinds of work.

8. Many modern improvements have been made in the construction of lenses and microscopes.

LOCATING SIDEHEADS

Reread the sideheads in the section "Sand to Glass to Lenses" or "The Microscopic World." Select one of the sideheads and read carefully the paragraph or paragraphs which follow it. Notice that the sidehead is the simplest kind of a summary.

Read the next selection, "The Distant World," to get a general idea of the article. Notice that there are blank lines instead of sideheads. Now reread the article carefully. Your PURPOSE for rereading is to place the following sideheads correctly. You will need to CONCENTRATE and watch for IMPORTANT DETAILS as you read to determine where each sidehead should be placed. *Take notes* to remind you of the location you have selected. Do not write in your book.

Sideheads

The street below
Resolving power
Telescopes—later uses
Measures—astronomical distances
Telescopes with a mirror
Observation—without a telescope

Light-gathering power
Telescopes—early uses
Binoculars
Telescopes with lenses

Now write the preceding sideheads in correct sequence. Indicate the page and paragraph where you located each sidehead. For example:

The street below—Page 298, Par. 1

Discuss your location of sideheads with your classmates. If there is disagreement on any of the locations, reread the necessary sections and try to find justification for *your* choice of location.

Now turn to the top of page 312 and summarize.

The Distant World

_____. From the observation deck of the Empire State Building we are looking down on a fascinating scene. The people on the street below appear to be not much larger than ants. The cars look like tiny toy models and look remarkably alike. They all seem to move together, as if they were on an endless belt. The traffic light changes. Some cars go and others stop. The "little people" scurry from curb to curb. The scene is an ant hill of going and coming, starting and stopping. We are captivated by all the activities below us.

Then the spell is broken. Suddenly we are curious about the policeman on the corner. What does he look like? Does he smile? Does he speak to the people passing by?

Curiously we turn to the binoculars mounted on the window sill of the skyscraper's observation deck. Binoculars are a kind of a telescope. We point the

binoculars toward the ground and peer through the eyepiece. Everything is blurred at first. We focus the binoculars, and the scene comes into view. Now everything is enlarged. We can easily see the policeman, his smile, and the way he nods his head to the people passing by.

_____. A pair of binoculars is a lens-using device that almost anyone would like to have. Binoculars are wonderful to use at a football game when the action is far away. Sailors use binoculars when they want to identify a distant ship or something floating in the water. Bird-watchers or judges of sailing boat races spend a great deal of time using binoculars.

Binoculars are usually described in such terms as 8x50 or 7x35. The first numeral is the magnification. The 8 means that when you are looking at something 160 yards away, the binoculars will let you see it as if it were one-eighth of that distance away. In this case you could see the object as if it were 20 yards away. What does the 7 in 7x35 mean?

The second numeral is the diameter of the objective lens in millimeters. This numeral tells about the lens's

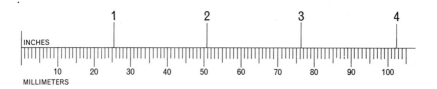

light-gathering power. The larger the lens the more light it can gather. What does the 50 in 8x50 mean? What does the 35 in 7x35 mean?

There could be a lens rated 7x25, another at 7x35, and another at 7x50. Each of the three lenses would give the same magnification, but the 7x25 wouldn't have much utility except in the full sunlight. The 7x35's usefulness would be diminished in the late afternoon and would end soon after sunset. The 7x50 could be used at night. So you see that there is more to consider than just magnification when you select binoculars. You also need to think about the light-gathering power of the binoculars. As a usual thing, a 7x35 binocular suits most people best.

_____. Looking through binoculars is much like looking through a large telescope. What would we know about our universe without telescopes? Just about as much as observant shepherds knew thousands of years ago. Some of them had to stay awake all night to watch their flocks. Without very much else to do, there was ample opportunity to watch the stars. They knew the paths the stars seemed to take as they crossed the sky at different times of the year. They knew that a few "stars" were probably not stars at all, because they moved in quite different patterns. These "stars" were planets, of course. The shepherds were familiar with meteors, but they were badly frightened by eclipses of the moon and by comets. These things were about all they could learn with their eyes alone. They didn't do anything very scientific with the information they had. But they invented stories and legends based on what they saw.

_____. The shepherds could see only about 3,000 separate stars with their unaided eyes, of all the billions upon billions of stars. Then along came Galileo with the first telescope that was put to scientific use.

Of course telescopes were improved as time went on, and many other instruments were developed to help men to interpret what the telescopes saw. Still, some early discoveries have not changed at all. About the year 1600, in Germany, a mathematician and astronomer named Johannes Kepler worked out a formula for calculating the orbits of all the planets in the solar system. His work has made it possible for today's scientists to put artificial earth satellites into fixed orbits. There was a very odd part of Kepler's life that shows how science and superstition can exist side by side. With the crude tools at his command, a mathematical genius like Kepler could figure out the orbits of planets—but his mother was put on trial accused of being a witch!

One of the first revelations of early telescopes was that the Milky Way, that river of light across our sky, is actually a mass of separate stars, and that our earth is a planet of one of the stars. Such a grouping of stars, like a city in space, is called a *galaxy*.

The galaxy in the constellation Andromeda

Later it became clear that almost all of the matter in the universe—the stars and planets and asteroids and dust and gases and comets and meteors—is organized into separate galaxies. Even after it was known that the universe, so far as we can see it, is made up of millions of galaxies, it once was thought that probably there was nothing at all in the space between them.

_____. Now the astronomers are aware that there are huge clouds of hydrogen gas, bits of matter, and various forms of radiation between the galaxies. It also seems that the galaxies may be in violent motion in directions that appear to be outward as seen from the earth. But all of these matters will need much more study, and much more use of telescopes, before we fully understand the universe.

_____. One thing that we must keep in mind about the universe is its size. Between galaxies are distances so vast that we cannot measure them in ordinary ways. There is an upper limit of speed in our universe. Nothing can move faster than the speed of light, which is 186,000 miles per second. This is the unit of distance once we get off our own little planet. Distances are measured in light-years— the distance light can travel in one year. The only way to begin to understand such vast distances is to compare them with something on earth. How long does it take light to get from one end of a football field to the other? It takes $\frac{1}{3,273,600}$ of a second— that is how long! It is no wonder that people say, "Light travels from one object on earth to another in an instant"!

Regulus, the brightest star in the constellation Leo, is about seventy-five light-years away from the earth. If Regulus should burn out on a boy's sixteenth birthday, how old would he be before the world would know that Regulus had burned out?

The moon on the average is 238,855 miles away from the earth. Light from the moon reaches us in about $1\frac{1}{3}$ seconds. The sun is farther away from the earth and its light reaches us in $8\frac{1}{2}$ minutes. Light from the nearest star reaches us in $4\frac{1}{2}$ years. Light traveling at 186,000 miles a second can go quite a distance in $4\frac{1}{2}$ years! The brightest star that we can see is Sirius, the Dog Star. Light from Sirius reaches us in a little less than 9 years.

We said that matter in the universe was organized into galaxies, and that the galaxies, although there are millions of them, are widely separated from each other. Well, then, how far away is the nearest galaxy that is something like our own? Two million light-years!

That is, we think the galaxy is still there. If we look through a telescope at it tonight, we must remember that the light that strikes our eyes left that galaxy two million years ago. But maybe the galaxy burst and burned out a million years ago. If so, it won't be known for another million years.

_____. What kinds of work do telescopes do? Our first thought is that they so greatly magnify the size of a distant star that we can see it better. Well, of course they do provide magnified images, but only up to a point. Even a large nearby planet, such as Venus, when seen through a telescope doesn't seem so very much larger than it is when seen with the unaided eye. But it is much brighter.

Find Orion's belt in both photographs. The telescope
shows many stars around and beyond Orion.

It is this ability to collect light from distant sources
that makes the big telescopes so valuable.

All of us know the constellation Orion, and especially the three bright stars that form the giant's
belt. To us they stand out sharply against a dark
background. But look at those three stars through a
good-sized telescope and they seem to be three somewhat brighter patches against an almost solid background of light. We cannot see the countless stars
that lie beyond Orion, but the telescope can.

Some of us have back-yard telescopes with lenses two inches across, or more. We know that the astronomers in the observatories have telescopes very much larger than that. Why is a bigger telescope better than a small one?

Any optical instrument, an eye or a telescope or a camera, can take in as much light as the diameter of its opening permits. Therefore, the wider the lens, the more light a telescope can take in for the use of the astronomer. You can keep on making bigger and bigger lenses, up to a point. Large lenses are very difficult to make. In the first place it is not easy to cast a large chunk of glass that is of uniform quality throughout. Then there is the fact that a lens is usually made not of one piece of glass but of several, each ground and polished to an exquisitely exact shape, size, and smoothness of surface so that each can be cemented together side by side to make a whole lens.

The largest telescope lens in existence is 40 inches across, and probably no larger one will ever be built. It is not that astronomers do not need "eyes" bigger than 40 inches in diameter. The fact is that larger lenses would be so heavy, and so difficult to make, that it would be out of the question to make them.

_____. Now imagine a telescope with a mirror used for the objective lens. In many ways it is easier to make a large mirror than it is to make a large lens. A telescope which uses a mirror is called a direct-focus reflector. Light comes in and strikes the inside of a saucer-shaped mirror. The reflected light will then come together or focus at the eyepiece. Both a mirror and a lens do the same things: gather light and bring it into focus. A mirror is not better than a lens in every way. But for reaching far out into space it *is* better.

The Hale Telescope on Mount Palomar in California is the world's largest reflecting telescope. Its mirror is 200 inches in diameter. It can show us the surface of the moon as if we were only 200 miles away. A secondary mirror can be used with the Hale Telescope, but some of its best sightings are made through direct focus.

An astronomer does some "direct sighting," but usually he works with photographic plates. The rays from the mirror are brought to focus on the plates and a picture is made of the star or galaxy being sighted. The Hale Telescope can photograph stars more than one billion light-years away!

_____. Great light-gathering power is a characteristic of the Hale Telescope and gives it far-seeing range. This light-gathering power is of more importance to astronomers than its magnifying power.

In looking at the moon or the sun the astronomer uses a magnifying telescope. He wants a close-up of the moon's plains or the sun's surface. But, in searching out stars, he is chiefly in need of light-gathering

The full moon

A portion of the moon's surface

power. Once the light is collected, there is no need to magnify the image. The light alone tells much about the star.

_____. Another important characteristic of a telescope is its *resolving* power. Resolving power is the ability of a telescope to separate objects in the sky. When we looked down at the policeman with our binoculars, everything was blurred until we brought him into focus. This resolving power or focusing power singled him out from the crowd below. To our unaided eyes, most stars appear to be single objects. But when viewed through a telescope, many spots of light show up as two or more stars.

Years ago Galileo cast his telescope on the Milky Way Galaxy. You can see it overhead on a moonless, summer night. It spreads across the sky like a white, milky veil. Galileo observed that the Milky Way is made up of many separate stars. His telescope resolved these stars into distinct objects. Our sun and all the planets comprise this galaxy.

Astronomers have discovered other galaxies within the universe. With far-seeing telescopes, they have located individual stars within these galaxies. They have looked back in time. The light from these stars actually came into existence millions of years ago.

The telescope is one of the scientist's most important tools. Without it, he could only marvel at the wonders of the universe. He could have little understanding of its scope and make-up. Through the telescope, he can observe space beyond our solar system. He can see light which started traveling millions of years ago. He can look backward into time and provide information which can be used in conquering space.

The last paragraph of "The Distant World" was a general summary of the entire article. When a summary is written, only basic ideas and concepts are included. Select one of the sideheads you have placed correctly and write a summary paragraph of that part of the article. Remember a summary is concise and includes only basic information. Share your summary with your classmates. If necessary they will give helpful suggestions for the improvement of your summary.

BUILDING MENTAL IMAGES

When you read about an event you have not witnessed, you sometimes feel as though you have really had experience with the event. An experience such as this is called a *vicarious* experience, and it is a substitute for an actual experience. Mental images that are stimulated by reading help you have vicarious experiences. Of course, actual experiences are best, but when they are impossible to have, vicarious experiences can increase your understanding and broaden your horizons.

How did the following statements help you BUILD MENTAL IMAGES?

1. To get an idea of what a half of a thousandth of an inch is, a human hair is *two or three thousandths* of an inch in diameter.

2. Another scientist might need presses so powerful that they could twist and mash steel beams as if they were made of straw.

3. Beneath the microscope, the [butterfly] wing takes on new beauty. It is seen to be a delicate web of neat rows of overlapping scales exactly like shingles on a roof.

4. The people on the street below appear to be not much larger than ants. The cars look like tiny toy models and look remarkably alike. They all seem to move together, as if they were on an endless belt.

5. It [the Milky Way] spreads across the sky like a white, milky veil.

DOING RESEARCH

The articles about the microscope and the telescope gave you some information concerning the parts of these tools. You were told how these tools work and something of the history of their development.

The next article, called "The Camera Records," will not give you information concerning the camera's parts and its history. The article deals entirely with some of the modern applications of the camera as a scientist's tool.

Before you read the next article, do some research on the camera. Find out about the various kinds of cameras and their uses. Learn about the fascinating history of the camera. Since this information is not in this book, you RECOGNIZE THE NEED FOR MORE INFORMATION. You know how to LOCATE INFORMATION OUTSIDE YOUR TEXT, so you are ready to go to work.

As you read from various sources, take notes to remind you of important facts you wish to remember. Keep a list of the sources you read. You may want to reread a source in order to compare information you obtain from a different source. Then use your notes to write a report about a topic you choose. Or perhaps you would like to make a report on one of these topics:

> The History of the Camera
> The Parts of a Camera
> Comparison: Camera and Eye
> The Polaroid Camera

When you present your report, you may want to use illustrations such as diagrams or charts to make your report more meaningful to your classmates. After you have given your report, give your classmates an opportunity to contribute additional information which they may have obtained from their reading. Also give them a chance to ask any questions they may have. As a result, you may need to do some additional research in order to answer these questions.

WRITING A LIST FOR A SUMMARY

Prepare to take notes as you read "The Camera Records." List in as few words as possible some of the modern uses of the camera today. An outline, a paragraph summary, and a list are *all* kinds of summaries.

The Camera Records

Like the microscope and the telescope, the camera helps the scientist see what the eye by itself cannot see. It also helps by making a record of what he has seen so he can study it at greater length later when he has more time.

Scientists use cameras in many ways and in many places. They use them alone and in combination with other scientific instruments such as microscopes and telescopes. They take pictures from the air, under the water, and inside of things, as well as from close range.

The photographic process is becoming increasingly useful to science and industry. It is also becoming increasingly useful to people for their own education and enjoyment.

Two modern applications of photography are remarkably alike in basic idea, but quite different in purpose. Pictures of the inside of a stomach have been made with a tiny camera apparatus at the end of a long tube. Pictures have been taken by archeologists of the interior of the underground Egyptian tombs by drilling a small hole in the roof and lowering a tiny camera apparatus at the end of a long tube. The purpose of the stomach photograph is to look for disease. The purpose of the tomb photograph is to see what is in the tomb without going to all the work of digging it out.

Aerial photographs are being used in many ways. Archeologists find that places where ancient peoples lived and worked can more easily be discovered from the air than from the ground. People about to develop new housing tracts, or establish new towns, or build new roads are very likely to start with aerial photographs. Public officials concerned with taxation can find taxable properties from the air that may not appear on the books at the courthouse. Cartographers now make use of aerial photographs when they make maps.

Things look different from the air. A farmer can use a field for years without ever suspecting that it

was an Indian camp site—a fact that shows up clearly on an aerial photograph. Earth once disturbed looks different from undisturbed terrain. Old fortifications and Indian mounds are clearly seen from the air, while anyone standing on the ground sees nothing but prairie.

You have probably seen X-ray pictures, but have you ever seen X-ray movies? Such a movie of the mouth and throat of a living person shows bones and teeth clearly, with flesh in shadowy outline. It is odd indeed to see a bite of apple being chewed and swallowed, or to see a girl apply lipstick to almost nonexistent lips.

Along with skin diving and scuba diving and underwater exploration has come an increased interest in

underwater photography. There is nothing especially different about it. You simply figure out some kind of enclosure that will keep water out of your camera and still let you set the controls. You also will need to bring lights under water with you if you are going to take pictures at any considerable depth. So far, undersea life has been photographed at depths of five miles. The pictures show facts that have surprised scientists and have triggered many new ideas.

One way in which a camera helps the scientist to see more than the eye alone can see is by *high-speed photography*. This makes it possible to see motions so rapid that the eye sees only a blur. Motion pictures can be made of fast actions, then the movies can be played back in slow motion. Scientists have taken

pictures of the way birds, bees, and many insects move their wings while flying. Men who design airplanes study these pictures, and thus birds and insects help man learn to fly.

If an engineer in a factory wants to know how a machine operates when it is turning hundreds of times a minute, he too makes use of high-speed photography. He can take photographs of a rapidly revolving wheel in such a way that, when the finished film is observed, the wheel seems to be standing still. Imagine that he has put a tiny white dot on the edge of the wheel. Imagine the wheel whizzing around and the dot arriving at the very top of its circular path with each revolution. Now suppose that at every tenth revolution the camera is set to take a photograph of the wheel when the dot is exactly at the top. Since he is photographing the wheel only in one position, it will seem not to be moving at all. Such a photograph can be used to discover imperfections in manufacture. Perhaps the wheel is vibrating, or it may be bending too much. When the engineer observes these things he can take steps to correct the imperfections.

Cameras are attached to the eyepieces of microscopes and become tools for many kinds of scientists. A man can focus his microscope on the surface of a piece of metal and take photographs while it is heated. This gives him a record he can study long after the metal has cooled.

A process called time-lapse photography has been of help to scientists. The process involves the taking of still pictures. The still pictures are then put together to form a motion picture of an event which occurred over a long period of time.

Doctors and medical students study time-lapse movies of the growth of bacteria. The growth of cells can be observed from movies made with cameras attached to microscopes.

Time-lapse photography has resulted in movies of great beauty. Movies of a flower opening or a snow crystal forming are lovely to see.

Time-lapse photography captures the unfolding of a gorgeous rose from bud to full-blown flower

When attached to telescopes, cameras record the position of stars invisible to the unaided eye. They can also show stars too distant even for direct viewing through a telescope. A film exposed for a long time builds up an image from the weak light rays of very distant stars and planets. Astronomers also use color photographs. Since different chemicals give off or reflect differing light rays, astronomers have learned something about the chemical make-up of heavenly bodies.

How else does a camera help us to see? We cannot see infrared rays (though we can feel them as heat if they are intense enough). But we know how to make photographic films sensitive to these rays. When these films are developed, scientists can see patterns made by heat rays. Infrared photographs taken from an airplane will show streets, buildings, parks and waterways of a city, even though the pilot looking down from the plane sees nothing but a seemingly impenetrable bank of fog.

Falsified paintings or documents can be photographed by infrared rays, too, and the picture will show brush strokes or letters invisible in ordinary light. The Dead Sea scrolls that were discovered near Jerusalem in 1948 were impossible to read at first. The scrolls had been lying in the cave since the first century A.D., and the letters had faded. But archeologists found that the scrolls were readable when infrared photographs were made.

Photographed with film
sensitive to light rays

Photographed with film sensitive to infrared rays

The invention of the camera has made it possible
for the scientist to probe inside of things where he
cannot see with his eyes alone; to slow down motion
so he can see what is happening; and to keep accurate records for further study. Inventions and im-

provements in the use of camera lenses and in film have given him valuable tools with which to work in his research.

Find out whether writing a list of the modern uses of cameras has helped you remember. Without using your list, see how many modern uses of the camera you can report. The other members of your group will listen without referring to their lists. If they can add to your report, they will do so.

Now compare your report, plus any additions which the group made, with your list. Were you successful in remembering the modern uses of the camera which were described in this article? If not, keep practicing this skill just as you practice other skills. Eventually you will find that note taking and writing various kinds of summaries will improve your power to remember what you have read.

Out of all of the scientists' tools, we have selected a few that involve the use of lenses. But we have not yet mentioned lenses that a great many scientists use, no matter in what field or science they work. Those are the lenses used in eyeglasses. Like all other lenses, eyeglass lenses take in light from one side and bend it in carefully measured ways as it passes through.

Eyeglasses have been used for a very long time. Perhaps the earliest reference to them in literature is part of a sermon preached in Italy, in 1306: "It is not twenty years since there was found the art of making eyeglasses which make for good vision, one of the best arts and most necessary that the world has."

NOTING SIMILARITIES AND DIFFERENCES

You have just finished reading about three very important tools used by scientists. They are all alike in one way: they all depend on lenses made of glass. But they are also different. One helps us see objects that are very small. One helps us see objects that are far away. And one helps us record what we have seen.

Each of the pairs of words below have some characteristics that are alike and other characteristics that are different. For each pair of words, state first how they are *similar*, then state how they are *different*.

artificial	*and*	natural
concave	*and*	convex
refraction	*and*	reflection
simple	*and*	compound
eyeglasses	*and*	telescopes
Leeuwenhoek	*and*	Galileo
microscopist	*and*	archeologist
hypothesis	*and*	guess
magnifying power	*and*	resolving power

binoculars	*and*	telescope
magnifying power	*and*	light-gathering power
light	*and*	electron

KNOWING MEANINGS OF WORD PARTS

As you know, many English words are formed from word parts adopted from other languages, especially Greek and Latin. Knowing the meaning of these word parts will help you increase your vocabulary. In the following list, the word parts followed by a hyphen are often found at the beginning or in the middle of English words (such as *magni-*). Or, if the word part is preceded by a hyphen, the word part is usually found in the middle or at the end of English words (such as *-fy*, or *-ation*). For example:

> *magni-* plus *-fy* makes *magnify* and means
>> to make large

> *magni-* plus *-fi* plus *-cation* forms
>> *magnification* and means
>> the result of making large

When you form English words from word parts, you will notice that slight changes in spelling need to be made. These changes are made because it is necessary to conform to established spelling patterns.

Useful Word Parts	Some Meanings
archeo-	ancient
bio-	life
etymo-	true meaning of a word judged by its origin
lingui-	tongue (language)
micro-	small
milli-	a thousandth
photo-	light
quali-	limit
techni-	skill
tele-	distant
thermo-	heat
-fy	to make
-graph	to write
-logy	to study the science of
-meter	to measure
-scope	to examine
-stat	to place in a fixed position
-ation	result of an action
-er	one who does
-ician	an expert in
-ist	one who specializes in

Use the meanings given for the word parts and tell the meaning of the underlined words in the following sentences:

1. Archeology is a hobby for some people.
2. Henry's father is a biologist.
3. John is studying to be a linguist.
4. We are enjoying our work in etymology.
5. A qualification of some of your statements is needed.
6. He will adjust the thermostat.
7. Carl Sandburg is a biographer of Lincoln.
8. The microscopist has been studying viruses.
9. The experiments were performed by a technician.
10. The scientist measured the size of the minute object in millimeters.
11. Mr. Taylor, an etymologist of renown, gave a speech on the true meaning of words.
12. The very thin groove on long-playing records is called a microgroove.

In this lesson on etymology, and in similar lessons in this book, you have learned an important way to increase your vocabulary. As your vocabulary increases, you understand more of what you read. If you continue to learn the meanings of word parts, it will help you become a better reader.

UNIT SEVEN

Reading Literature

RECOGNIZING FACT AND FICTION

Scientists are interested in reporting facts, because they want to give you information. But the person whose purpose is to entertain you need not deal in facts. His writings are called *fiction*.

Long before people could read, they told each other stories. Even if a story was originally true, it gradually changed with each retelling until some or all of the story became fiction. This type of fiction is called a *legend*.

Legends, such as those concerning King Arthur, sometimes mix history with fiction. There may have been a King Arthur living in England in the fifth or sixth century, but in many of the stories about him things occur in a magical way. Long ago people believed that the magical happenings which were reported in the legends were based on facts. Today careful readers are sure that they are fictional.

A good reader strives to develop the ability to distinguish the difference between fact and fiction. As you read the legend about King Arthur, decide which parts you think are fact and which are fiction. Keep a list of your decisions. Use context clues to help you understand unusual expressions. Later you will read a factual account of knighthood, and you can then compare the two types of writing.

The Pulling of the Sword

In the days when King Uther Pendragon ruled over England, a baby was born to him and his queen. Now the king fell ill and Merlin, the mighty magician, knew he would soon die. Then powerful nobles might kill the little prince so they could have the kingdom for themselves. Therefore, Merlin placed the baby under the care of Sir Ector, a faithful subject, until the child was old enough to take care of himself. No one, not even Sir Ector, was told the boy was of royal birth. The child was named "Arthur."

When Merlin thought Arthur was old enough, he went to the Archbishop of Canterbury and counseled him to call all the lords to London on Christ-

mas day, so God might show by some miracle which one should become king. It was believed the king must be divinely chosen. On that day a huge marble stone appeared in the churchyard. In the midst thereof was an anvil of steel one foot high with a beautiful sword in it. On the sword was written,

"Whoso pulleth out this sword from this stone and anvil, is rightful king of all England."

When they saw the words, many tried, but none could move the sword.

"The man is not here," said the Archbishop, "who will win the sword, but soon God will make him known to us. This is my counsel, that ten knights of good fame be left here to guard the sword." So it was ordained.

On New Year's Day the barons held a tournament so that everyone could be brought together and afterwards could try to remove the sword.

Now it happened that Arthur, Sir Ector, and Sir Kay, his son, rode to the jousts. As Sir Kay was getting ready, he saw that he had forgotten his sword and asked Arthur to ride back after it.

This Arthur did, but when he found no one home to give it to him he rode to the churchyard; and finding the sentries at the jousting, Arthur lightly and fiercely pulled the sword from the stone.

As soon as Sir Kay saw the sword, he recognized it. He rode to his father and said, "Sir, look! Here is the sword of the stone. I must be king of this land." When Sir Ector saw the sword, he led Arthur and Sir Kay back to the churchyard. He made Sir Kay swear on a book saying how he got the sword. "Sir," said Sir Kay, "my brother Arthur brought it to me."

"How did ye get this sword, Arthur?" asked Sir Ector.

"Sir, when I went home for my brother's sword, I found everyone had gone to the jousting. As I thought my brother should not be swordless, I went to the churchyard and easily pulled out this sword from the unguarded stone."

"Now," said Sir Ector, "I understand ye must be king of this land. But let us see if ye can replace the sword and pull it out again."

Arthur replaced the sword quickly. Then both Sir Ector and Sir Kay assayed to pull out the sword and failed.

"Now I shall assay," said Arthur, and he pulled it out easily. At once Sir Ector and Sir Kay kneeled down on the ground before Arthur.

"Alas," cried Arthur, "my own dear father and brother, why do ye kneel to me?"

"Nay, my lord, I was never your father, but I see ye are of higher blood than I thought ye were." Then Sir Ector told him how Merlin, the wise magician, had asked him to take care of the baby.

"I make great dole," Arthur cried, when he learned Sir Ector was not his father.

"Sir," said Sir Ector to Arthur, "will ye be good to us when ye are made king?"

"If it is God's will that I be king," said Arthur, "whatever ye ask of me I shall not fail you."

"Sir," said Sir Ector, "I will ask no more of you but that ye make my son, your foster brother, seneschal of all your lands."

"That shall be done," said Arthur.

On the twelfth day after the New Year, all the barons again came to London to assay the sword, but only Arthur could remove it. At this all the lords were angry and said, "It would be a great shame to us to be governed by a boy who has no royal blood." So they delayed twice more, with the same result. Finally they put it off until the Feast of Pentecost.

On that day, on Merlin's advice, all the best knights assayed to pull out the sword, but none succeeded except Arthur, who pulled it out before all the lords and commons. All the common people cried, "We will have Arthur for our king; we won't delay him any longer. We see it is God's will that he be our king. We will slay anyone who still denies Arthur his right."

Then they all knelt down and cried to Arthur, "Mercy, because we have delayed thee so long."

"Mercy, ye shall have," said Arthur, and he took the sword and placed it on the altar so he could be made a knight by the best man there. Then he was crowned king by the Archbishop. The young king vowed to be a true king and uphold justice as long as he lived.

Then the lords and commons shouted together, "Long live King Arthur! Long live the King!"

Much wrong had been done in the realm since the death of King Uther, and Arthur at once began to right these wrongs. Merlin became his chief adviser, and as King Arthur had promised, he made Sir Kay the seneschal of all England.

Compare your list of fact and fiction with your classmates' lists. Discuss any points of disagreement you may have. After you have read the selection on "The Training of a Knight," you probably will have factual information which will settle most of your disagreements.

READING CRITICALLY

The word *critical* has several meanings. If we say "Mary is a critical person," we probably mean she finds fault. But if we say "Mary is a critical reader," we mean she uses judgment as she reads. She examines everything the author has to say and then compares this with what she knows and with what other sources say.

An author may report factual information in several ways. He may write it in the form of a story recounting an actual event, such as Perry's account of his trip to the North Pole. Or, if he wishes to inform you about a certain subject, he may write an essay.

The article that follows is an essay. The author informs you on the subject of "The Training of a Knight." This is not an account of a particular knight's experiences, but is a discussion of the topic in general. The essay is one way of presenting facts.

When reading for facts, it is important to know something about the source. The author of "The Training of a Knight" has studied history for a long time and has carefully checked his facts. A critical reader checks the author's facts by listing them and then reading other articles on the subject to see if all the facts agree.

Read the essay and list the facts stated.

The Training of a Knight

The story of knights and knighthood and the Age of Chivalry is a curious blend of fact and fiction—of life as it really existed in the England and France of nearly a thousand years ago, and as it has been handed down to us through the creative imagination of poets and storytellers.

This is the story of the knights—how they lived, and fought, and sometimes died.

At the beginning of the Age of Chivalry there were no organized governments. Nobles and overlords each had their own tiny kingdoms, centered around a huge stone castle. They had their knights —who were the select group of fighting men, comparable to the officers of a modern army—and the foot soldiers and archers, who were the "privates."

Each noble also had his serfs, or peasants, who tilled his lands and kept his herds. In return for their work, the nobles and knights protected them. Knighthood legends grew out of this duty of the knights to protect the weak and the poor.

The nobles were almost constantly at war with each other, attacking the castles of their rivals to rob and loot, and in defense of their own properties. For this reason, the knights were trained primarily as fighting men, ready to protect the property of their lords from the frequent raids of neighboring lords and wandering bands.

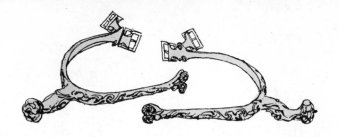

As time went on, groups of neighboring nobles banded together for mutual protection. The richest and strongest among them—the one who had the most knights and the largest army of foot soldiers—became "king," and the other nobles pledged their loyalty to him. But fighting continued as "kingdoms" went to war against each other.

At last, in the natural course of events, the various "kings" banded together or were conquered by their rivals, until each country had but one king. This was the beginning of organized national government and also of large-scale wars between countries, such as those that raged for a great many years between England and France.

Most knights were the sons of kings, princes, barons, and other knights. They started their training for knighthood early in life, usually about the age of seven. While they were learning, they earned their keep as pages, running errands, caring for the knights' armor, and waiting on table in the great hall of their master's castle. Meanwhile, they went to school. Here, instead of learning to read and write, which was not considered a proper occupation for knights, they learned to ride, to fight with wooden swords and lances, to wrestle and to run.

The training of a page went on until he was about fourteen years old. Then, if his teachers were satisfied that he might someday make a good knight, he was promoted to the rank of squire. He was assigned as the personal servant to a knight, caring for his master's armor, his war horse and his weapons. And now, instead of a wooden sword, he carried a real one with which he practiced every day.

The knights took great pride in the progress made by their squires and taught them all they knew about the art of warfare. Sometimes, in battle, the squires formed a second line of defense behind the knights.

When a squire reached the age of twenty-one,

he was ready to become a knight. But before he could win his spurs, which was a symbol of knighthood, he had to prove himself by some feat of bravery or skill at arms.

In spite of their rugged life and love of fighting, the knights and nobles were religious in their own fashion. And the making of a knight was a solemn occasion. The squire spent the night before the ceremony praying in a church. In the morning, he bathed and put on a white robe. After a long sermon by the priest, the ceremony of knighting began.

Dressed in a new suit of armor, the squire knelt before his king or overlord. Drawing his sword, the king struck the young man lightly on the shoulder

with its blade and proclaimed: "In the name of God, Saint Michael and Saint George, I dub thee knight!"

Sometimes, when he had performed some particularly brave deed in battle, a squire was rewarded by being knighted on the spot. It was a great honor to win a knight's spurs in this way. The new knight was addressed as "Sir," a squire was appointed to attend him, and he was allowed to choose his own insignia, or coat of arms.

This custom has come down to modern times. Soldiers who have distinguished themselves in action are often awarded commissions right on the battlefield.

TESTING FACTUAL ACCURACY

As you read "The Training of a Knight," you kept a list of the facts stated. Therefore, as a critical reader, you will want to check these facts. One way of testing factual accuracy is to read from several other sources and compare your list of facts with what other authors say.

First make a list of questions about the statements in "The Training of a Knight" that you wish to check. Under each, write the answer given in the essay.

Second, for each reference you read, write the answer given by that source as well as the title, author, and page number of it.

Third, reread the several answers for each question and see if you can verify the statements made in the essay.

You may use the following questions, and you may wish to add some of your own.

1. How long did a page's training take?
2. How long did a squire's training take?
3. What were the duties of a page?
4. What were the duties of a squire?
5. How did the squire spend the night before he became knighted?
6. What ceremonies did he go through on the day he was knighted?

READING SATIRE

After 1500, no one lived in the way described in "The Training of a Knight." Yet for one hundred years longer people continued to take knighthood seriously. Books about chivalry were very popular.

In about 1600, Miguel de Cervantes wrote a fictional satire on knighthood. A satire ridicules something. Cervantes makes fun of Don Quixote because he tried to live like a knight in a time when no one else did. Cervantes was telling his readers that they were foolish to dream about one way of life when they were living another way.

A satire often attempts to change the way people behave or think. Cervantes' satire did change the reading tastes of the people of his time. They stopped reading books about chivalry. Authors even stopped writing books about it.

We still enjoy the legends Cervantes laughed at, but we enjoy the story of Don Quixote, too. It was one of the first long stories other than a legend that was written in prose. The book from which the next story was taken has been called the grandfather of the novel. A novel is an original story with characters and a plot which is long enough to fill one or more books. Some novels are imaginary and some are based on facts.

As you read, make notes of the things Cervantes ridiculed.

An Adventure of Don Quixote

In a village in Spain there once lived a gentle-man of rather small means. Stew on weekdays, soup on Saturday, and a pigeon or so on Sunday took three-fourths of his money. With the rest of his income he was able to pay a housekeeper to look after his needs, to buy a fine suit of clothes for holidays, and to buy another suit for everyday. His age bordered on fifty. He was a lean man, a very early riser, and a lover of the chase. His name was Quixote.

Quixote gave himself up to the reading of books on chivalry. He even sold his land to buy books about knighthood. Soon all the legends and fancies that he read seemed true to him, more true than history itself. He read night and day, and what with little sleep and much reading his brains got so dry that he lost his wits.

He hit upon the strangest notion that ever a madman in this world hit upon. He fancied that he should become a knight, righting every wrong, facing danger, and winning lasting fame for his bravery. Led astray by the pleasure he took in these fancies, he set himself upon the road to knighthood.

The first thing he did was try to clean up some tarnished armor that had belonged to his great-grandfather. He scoured and polished it as best he could, but it had no helmet to protect his head. Never mind, he made himself one of cardboard. To see if it were strong enough, he slashed it with his sword, thus cutting to pieces in an instant the helmet it had taken him a week to make. He made another with iron bars inside the cardboard. Not caring to try any more experiments, he convinced himself that it was a perfect helmet and tied it to his head with a piece of green ribbon.

His broken-down old nag began to look like a prancing war horse to him. He named the old nag Rosinante, thinking this a romantic name for the steed of the knight Don Quixote.

Next, since every knight needed a lady to love, he settled on a simple farm girl. Her name, too, had to be changed to fit his absurd fancy, and he chose the name Dulcinea. So far as is known, the

girl never gave him a thought, but he easily persuaded himself of her love.

He sallied forth one morning, clad in his armor, with his helmet tied to his head and a lance and buckler in his hands. Scarcely did he reach the open country when a terrible thought struck him. He had not yet been knighted! But his craze was stronger than reason. He made up his mind to have

himself knighted by the knight of the first castle
he came across, and he rode on letting his horse
wander where it wished.

Toward nightfall both he and his nag were faint
with hunger. Fortunately, they came upon an inn,
which Don Quixote thought was a castle. Two
women standing by the door were frightened at
the strange sight of the knight, but he raised his cardboard visor and addressed them thus, "Your lady-
ships need not fear any rudeness, for it belongs not
to the order of knighthood to offer rudeness to
anyone, much less to highborn ladies." The simple
girls screamed with laughter upon hearing themselves called highborn ladies, and their laughter
attracted the keeper of the inn. He came out of the
door and would have laughed too, except that he
felt threatened by the sword and lance in the crazed
knight's hands.

"Sir Knight," he said, "will you spend the night
in my inn?"

"Aye, mighty owner of the castle," replied Don
Quixote, "forsooth I will lie here this night."

The giggling girls helped him get out of his armor, but they could not untie the ribbon that held his helmet. He would not allow them to cut the ribbon, and insisted on eating dinner with the helmet on his head. This was difficult to do, even when he held up the cardboard visor, and he had to drink through a straw.

Having finished supper, he fell on his knees before the innkeeper, saying, "From this spot I rise not, valiant knight, until you grant me the boon I seek."

The keeper stared at him in bewilderment and begged him to rise, but Don Quixote refused to do so until his boon was granted. "Knight me tomorrow morning," he begged. "Tonight I shall watch my arms in the chapel of your castle. After you knight me, I shall roam the four corners of the earth seeking adventure, rescuing maidens in distress, and doing great deeds of chivalry."

By now the landlord was well aware that his guest had lost his wits. As a joke, he agreed to knight him the next morning. "We have torn down the old chapel," he said, "because we are building a new one. You will have to watch your arms in the barnyard."

So Don Quixote collected his armor and placed it in the watering trough in the barnyard. Holding his lance in one hand and his buckler in the other, he marched up and down before it. Mean-

while, the keeper went back to the inn and laughingly told his guests about the crazy knight.

One of the stableboys came to let the horses drink from the trough. As the boy began to move the armor out of the way, Don Quixote called in a loud voice, "Thou knight that comest to lay hands on the armor of the brave Don Quixote, touch it not unless thou wouldst surrender thy life."

The stableboy paid no attention, but threw the armor on the ground. Don Quixote raised his eyes to the sky and cried, "Aid me, Lady Dulcinea, in this my first ominous adventure!" And he lifted his lance with both hands and gave the stableboy such a blow that the boy fell to the ground in a daze.

But other stableboys had seen all this, and they began angrily throwing stones at Don Quixote. "Lady of Beauty," he cried, "turn thy eyes on this thy knight on the brink of so mighty an adventure." This excited him so that he would not have been afraid of an army of stableboys, and he began striking first here, then there, with his sword.

The innkeeper, attracted by the noise, shouted to the boys to leave him alone, for he had already told them the man was mad. He decided it was time to put an end to the joke. After calming Don Quixote, he offered to knight him immediately, hoping to get rid of him.

"I stand ready to obey, Sir Knight," announced Don Quixote.

The landlord struck the kneeling knight on the shoulder with the sword, and the two girls who had first seen him helped him dress in his heavy armor and saddle Rosinante. The innkeeper, glad to be rid of him, boosted the knight up on the horse.

Don Quixote raised his sword in farewell. The nag, weighted down with so much armor, shuffled toward the road. Thus began the adventures of the famous knight Don Quixote.

Use your notes and give an oral summary of the things Cervantes ridiculed.

FINDING REAL TRAITS
IN FICTIONAL CHARACTERS

Even though fiction does not have to deal with facts, fiction is often called "true to life." Fictional characters may seem as real to you as do your own friends. People in a story are people you like, or dislike, people who arouse your sympathy or your laughter. You can discuss traits in their characters just as you can discuss the traits of real people.

Find points in the legend, essay, and satire to support the following statements about character traits:

1. Don Quixote was impractical and highly imaginative.

2. Sir Kay was vain, selfish, and dishonest.

3. Arthur was humble and modest.

4. Sir Ector was honest and trustworthy.

5. Merlin was ingenious.

6. The landlord in "An Adventure of Don Quixote" had a sense of humor.

CLARIFYING FACT AND FICTION

You have read examples of some types of factual and fictional writing. The following pages will help you review these literary types. You will find three selections concerning the sport of jousting as it was performed in the Age of Chivalry. First you will find a factual article written in the form of an essay. Then you will read two fictional excerpts, one written as a legend and the other as a satire.

The author of the essay will adhere to facts. While the fictional selections will have a realistic setting, the legend will include imaginary aspects and the satire will emphasize the ridiculous.

As you read these selections, compare the ways in which the discussion of jousting is presented, and determine how much of the fictional excerpts is based on facts. If you read critically, you should be able to recognize the different types of writing and explain what makes one an essay, one a legend, and the other a satire.

Jousting

In the Middle Ages, kings and their knights used several forms of fighting. One method involved a battle, called *jousting*, between two knights on horseback. There were two kinds of jousts—one was peaceful and one was serious.

Peaceful jousts were held both as social events and as training for warfare. Two mounted knights sheathed in heavy armor waited at opposite ends of an enclosed field. At the blare of a trumpet they charged, riding through narrow lanes, separated from each other by railings so that the horses did not meet.

Each knight, following prescribed rules of courtesy, tried to unseat his opponent. Because they were skillful, blood was seldom shed.

In a serious joust one knight might challenge another in a battle to the death or exhaustion. The challenge might result because each was from a different country, or because one knight felt the other had dishonored him. Perhaps a knight wanted to help a comrade or defend a lady. The winner could slay his opponent or show his chivalry by turning his rival over to a lady to free or to have slain.

Because people loved the sport, in western Europe jousting survived chivalry itself.

How Enchantment Caused a Combat

One day while they were hunting in a great forest, King Arthur and one of his knights, Sir Accolon, fell under an enchantment. Arthur was made to joust in place of a coward, who was a cruel man. Sir Accolon was to take the place of the coward's brother. Thus, through enchantment, King Arthur and Sir Accolon were to fight each other and neither would know who the other was.

At the signal of the trumpet, the two knights faced each other from opposite sides of the field and let their horses run so fast that each threw the other from his horse. They continued the battle on foot until Arthur got the better of Sir Accolon. Finally the veil of enchantment was raised enough so they could recognize each other.

All the people fell down on their knees and begged for mercy. "Mercy ye shall have," said Arthur. "Here ye see what adventures come to knights by enchantments, for I have fought one of my own knights."

Then Arthur gave the coward's lands to the brother, who had nothing to do with the enchantments. "A fitting punishment shall surely come to all evildoers," said King Arthur. Then he made the brother one of his own knights.

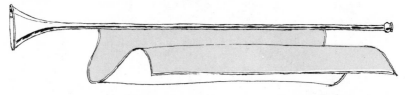

The Rescue of the Princess

As Don Quixote was riding along, he saw two monks on mules, followed by a coach carrying a lady. He thought, "Surely those two dark things moving towards me are magicians, carrying away by force a princess in that coach. 'Tis my duty to prevent this." He stopped his horse in front of the monks, saying, "Release that highborn princess or prepare to meet instant death."

Without waiting for a reply, he spurred Rosinante so furiously towards one that, had the monk not thrown himself on the ground, he would have been killed. The other monk then scurried his mule over the plain as if he had been running a race with the wind. The fallen monk, scared out of his wits, got on his mule and spurred after his friend.

A squire riding behind the lady shouted to Don Quixote to leave or be killed. At that Don Quixote drew his sword. Both grabbed cushions from the coach for shields and then began to joust. Finally the squire lost his stirrups and let go of his mule, who galloped wildly over the field. The squire was thrown to the ground, stunned.

"Lady," said Don Quixote, "at your request I grant this fellow his life on condition that he appear before my lady, Dulcinea, that she may dispose of him as pleases her." The terrified lady agreed, and the party resumed its journey.

THINKING BACK

You have read carefully the selection about jousts. Answer the following questions correctly, and you will show growth in your ability to read critically.

a. As you know, the legend on page 360 and the satire on page 361 were fictional selections. However, authors of fiction often use factual statements in their writing. What statements in the legend and the satire can be verified as factual when compared with the essay on pages 358 and 359?

b. What part or parts of the legend were purely imaginary?

c. What parts of the satire ridiculed someone or something?

To show that you now understand the forms of literature discussed, write three paragraphs of your own on one topic of the Age of Chivalry. Write a factual essay on your topic. Then portray the same information in a legend. Finally, rewrite it in the form of a satire. You may select your own area of study or choose one listed below:

   a. Tournaments
   b. Equipment of a Knight
   c. Rules of Courtesy
   d. Banner of a Knight
   e. The Age of Chivalry
   f. The Sport of Falconry

SAYING IT ANOTHER WAY

Father said, "We motored down the new highway at a speed in excess of a mile a minute."

Louise said, "We drove down the new road over sixty miles an hour."

They both expressed the same idea. Each one said it in a different way. See if you can say the same thing in still another way.

The authors who wrote the legends, essays, and satires used some unusual expressions. Many of them are not the way you would express the same idea. Find the following expressions in this unit. See if you can say each expression in another way.

Page 334, In the midst thereof

Page 334, ten knights of good fame

Page 334, So it was ordained.

Page 335, rode to the jousts

Page 335, assayed to pull out the sword

Page 336, I make great dole.

Page 336, seneschal of all your lands

Page 348, of rather small means

Page 351, sallied forth

Page 352, forsooth I will lie here this night

Page 358, sheathed in heavy armor

Page 360, fell under an enchantment

Page 361, spurred after his friend

UNDERSTANDING THE PLOT OF A STORY

Every fictional story has a plan or a plot. The events happen sometime and somewhere. A problem is introduced. Something happens. The events become more and more exciting until they reach a peak, or climax. Then the story ends, usually in a satisfying manner.

An example of a plot outline follows:

The Pulling of the Sword

I. Setting—England in the Age of Chivalry
II. Problem—A lawless country without a king
III. Action—A search for a king
IV. Climax—Arthur was crowned king
V. Outcome—Law and order was restored

By adding a few words to this plot outline, it becomes a summary. For example:

England in the Age of Chivalry *was* a lawless country without a king. A search for a king *followed*. Arthur was crowned king *and* law and order was restored.

As a critical reader you will want to test this plot outline on other stories. Then, by adding a few words or changing their form, see if you can write your plot outline as a summary.

Now that you have finished this book, bring to mind once more the skills that you used in reading

From Coins to Kings. All of your reading will be more useful and enjoyable if you will remember to:

1. CONCENTRATE.
2. KNOW YOUR PURPOSE.
3. KNOW THE MEANING AND THE PRONUNCIATION OF EVERY WORD.
    a. Use context clues.
    b. Use glossary or a dictionary.
    c. Use structure clues.
    d. Know word history.
4. FIT YOUR SPEED TO YOUR NEEDS.
5. KNOW WHAT YOU READ.
    a. Take notes.
    b. Make an outline.
    c. Write a summary.
6. READ TO UNDERSTAND RELATIONSHIPS.
7. BUILD MENTAL IMAGES.
8. RECOGNIZE IMPORTANT DETAILS.
9. RECOGNIZE WHEN RESEARCH IS NECESSARY AND MAKE USE OF RESEARCH SKILLS.
10. READ CRITICALLY.

Words are "coins of the realm" in literature, and, as you improve your reading, all of you can become kings of that realm!

The pronunciation key will help you to understand what the diacritical marks mean.

The principal, or heavy, accent is indicated by the mark ′ after a syllable. In some words another syllable is also accented, but not so heavily. Such a syllable has the mark ′ after it — called a secondary accent.

a as in hat	o as in hot	th as in thin
ā as in āge	ō as in ōpen	ŦH as in then
ã as in cãre	ô as in ôrder	
ä as in fäther		zh as in measure
	oi as in oil	
e as in let	ou as in house	ə represents:
ē as in ēqual		a in about
ėr as in tėrm	u as in cup	e in taken
	u̇ as in fu̇ll	i in pencil
i as in it	ü as in rüle	o in lemon
ī as in īce	ū as in ūse	u in circus

Glossary

a

a- (*prefix*), on; in; to

ab′a cus (ab′ə kəs), a frame used for counting with rows of beads that slide on wires

ab′stract (ab′strakt), not realistic; a design rather than a picture of an object

ab surd′ (ab sėrd′), foolish; silly

ac′cent (ak′sent), a different way of pronouncing words; a mark to show which syllable of a word to stress in pronunciation

A.D., the initials which stand for the Latin words meaning "In the year of our Lord"; used to designate the number of years *after* the birth of Christ in indicating dates

ad here′ (ad hēr′), stick to

ad ver′si ty (ad vėr′sə ti), bad luck

aer′i al (ãr′i əl), from the air; in the air

al′tar (ôl′tər), raised platform for worship

al′ter (ôl′tər), change; revise

---

al tim′e ter (al tim′ə tər), an instrument for measuring altitude or height

am′ple (am′pəl), plenty; more than enough

an′ces tor (an′ses tər), parent, grandparent, great-grandparent, and so on back through all generations of a family

an′gle (ang′gəl), turn; bend

an′vil (an′vəl), a block of iron or steel on which metal is hammered and shaped

ap′pa ra′tus (ap′ə rā′təs), equipment; tools for a certain task

ap pend′age (ə pen′dij), something added

ap pen′dix (ə pen′diks), explanatory material at the end of a book; a growth fastened to some part of the body

aq′ua lung′ (ak′wə lung′), a breathing device used underwater

ar′che ol′o gist (är′ki ol′ə jist), a scientist who studies the remains of cities and other records of ancient human life

ar′chi pel′a go (är′kə pel′ə go), a group or cluster of small islands in the sea

ar′chi tec′ture (är′kə tek′chər), art or science of building

ar′id (ar′id), dry

ar′ti fi′cial (är′tə fish′əl), not natural; man-made

as′pect (as′pekt), one part or idea

as say′ (ə sā′), try; test

as sume′ (ə süm′), take for granted; accept as true

as tound′ (əs tound′), amaze; astonish; surprise

aus′pi ces (ôs′pə siz), under the direction of; sponsorship; support

aye (ī), yes

az′ure (azh′ər), blue in color; the color of the sky

b

bac te′ri a (bak tēr′i ə), tiny one-celled plants, usually seen only through a microscope

bade (bad), told; ordered

ba′sic (bā′sik), important; essential

ba′sis (bā′sis), main part; foundation

bath′y scaphe (bath′ə skāf), underwater boat used to explore the deep sea

B.C., the initials which stand for the words "Before Christ"; used to designate the number of years *before* the birth of Christ in indicating dates

boon (bün), favor; request

bot′a ny (bot′ə ni), a study of plant life

boul′e vard (bül′ə värd), a wide street

brink (bringk), beginning; edge

buck′ler (buk′lər), a shield used for protection

buf′fet (buf′it), push about forcefully

c

cal′cu late (kal′kū lāt), figure out

cal'o rim'e ter (kal'ə rim'ə ter), an instrument for measuring heat

cap size' (kap sīz'), overturn

cap'ti vate (kap'tə vāt), fascinate; hold great interest in

car'cass (kär'kəs), the dead body of an animal

car'go (kär'gō), the load carried by the ship

cast (kast), throw; to throw in a certain direction; mold

cat'a logue (kat'ə lôg), a list of items in a collection

cen ten'ni al (sen ten'i əl), anniversary of 100 years

chal'lenge (chal'ənj), something to prove; contest or invitation to a contest

chiv'al ry (shiv'əl ri), gallant action; courtesy

chlo'rine (klô'rēn), a chemical substance used to purify water by killing harmful bacteria

chro nom'e ter (krə nom'ə tər), an instrument for measuring time

col lide' (kə līd'), crash into; bump; hit

col'or (kul'ər), to shade; to tint; also a hue or tint

col'ors (kul'ərz), flag; banner

com'pe ti'tion (kom'pə tish'ən), rivalry; attempt to win or excel

com prise' (kəm prīz'), make up; compose

con cise' (kən sīs'), brief; exact

con flict' (kən flikt'), disagree

con form' (kən fôrm'), fit; adapt to a pattern

con'shelf (kon'shelf), a word formed from the words "continental shelf," an underwater plain bordering a continent

con'stel la'tion (kon'stə lā'shən), a cluster of stars or heavenly bodies

cor'al (kôr'əl), hard substance made up of skeletons of tiny sea animals

cor'al - en crust'ed (kôr'əl en-krust'id), covered with a hard shell or crust of coral

cor rob'o rate (kə rob'ə rāt), to make more certain that something is true

cor rode' (kə rōd'), eat away slowly

coun'sel (koun'səl), suggest; advise

coun'te nance (koun'tə nəns), face; facial expression

crag (krag), a steep cliff; a rocky ledge

cred'it (kred'it), honor; recognition

cres'cent (kres'ənt), shaped like a new moon

crev'ice (krev'is), a narrow opening

cringe (krinj), draw back in fear; shrink

crude (krüd), simple; unrefined

---

hat, āge, cãre, fäther; let, ēqual, tėrm; it, īce; hot, ōpen, ôrder; oil; house; cup, fůll, rüle, ūse; th, thin; ᴛʜ, then; zh, measure; ə represents *a* in about, *e* in taken, *i* in pencil, *o* in lemon, *u* in circus

cur'rent (kėr'ənt), a flow of water, wind, electricity; the present time

curt'ly (kėrt'li), rudely and briefly

cut'tle fish' (kut'əl fish'), a sea animal with ten arms and a hard, internal shell; related to the octopus, and it ranges in size from a few inches to six feet long

cy lin'dri cal (sə lin'drə kəl), round with flat ends, shaped like a can

dole (dōl), sadness; grief; sorrow

Don (don), Spanish title similar to "Mr." or "Sir"

don (don), to put on

Dra'ma Club (drä'mə klub), a group of people who perform plays

dread (dred), have great fear

dry'ly (drī'li), in a rather sarcastic way

dub (dub), pronounce; name; give a title to

du'ra ble (dür'ə bəl), strong; lasting

d

daw'dle (dô'dəl), waste time

de bate' (di bāt'), consider; discuss reasons for or against

dec'i mal (des'ə məl), a tenth part; a number system based on a unit of 10

de prive' (di prīv'), without the use of

de vise' (di vīz'), work out; plan

di am'e ter (dī am'ə tər), a straight line through the center of a circle or a sphere

dig'it (dij'it), a single figure; one of the numerals from 0 to 9

di min'ish (də min'ish), lessen; reduce

dip'lo mat'ic (dip'lə mat'ik), able to say and do the right things

di verge' (də verj'), spread apart or move in different directions

doc'u ment (dok'u mənt), record or paper furnishing proof of a fact

dol'drums (dol'drəmz), calm seas with little or no wind

e

e- (*prefix*), out of; from

e clipse' (i klips'), a darkening of the moon or sun when a heavenly body is in position to cut off its light

e'co nom'i cal (ē'kə nom'ə kəl), avoid waste; plan carefully

e lec'tro mag'net (i lek'trō mag'nit), a magnet made by passing electric current through a wire around a piece of iron

e lec'tron (i lek'tron), an invisible charge of negative electricity; part of an atom

e lim'i nate (i lim'ə nāt), omit

em'er ald (em'ər əld), a precious stone that is bright-green in color

e merge' (i merj'), come into view

e mit' (i mit'), give off

em'pire (em'pīr), kingdom; lands to rule

en chant'ment (en chant'mənt), magic spell; supernatural force

en com′pass (en kum′pəs), surround; enclose on all sides

en′sign (en′sĭn), banner or flag

e′qua to′ri al (e′kwə tô′ri əl), near the equator

es′say (es′ā), a short literary composition on a certain subject, in which the author explains something

et′y mol′o gy (et′ə mol′ə ji), the scientific study of the origin and history of words

ev′i dent (ev′ə dənt), very clear; understandable

ex act′ (eg zakt′), carefully chosen; accurate

ex alt′ (eg zôlt′), honor

ex′cerpt (ek′sèrpt), part selected from the whole, as a passage from a book

ex pose′ (eks pōz′), open to the weather; permit light to reach and act on film

ex′qui site (eks′kwi zit), as perfect as possible

f

fa′ble (fā′bəl), story which teaches a lesson

fac′tor (fak′tər), a condition which brings about a result; any of the numbers which when multiplied produce a given number

fal′con ry (fôl′kən ri), a sport which uses birds called falcons for hunting

far′-fetched′ (fär′fecht′), exaggerated; highly imaginative

feat (fēt), an action that is brave or unusual

fil′a ment (fil′ə mənt), a fine wire that will glow when heated

flood′light′ (flud′līt′), a wide artificial beam that floods an area with light

flu′o res′cent (flü′ə res′ənt), containing a substance that gives off light when exposed to certain rays

flur′ried ly (flèr′id li), in a hurry; flittingly

fo′cus (fō′kəs), bring to a point; sharpen the image

for′mu la (fôr′mū lə), recipe; directions for doing something

fre′quent (frē′kwənt), often; at close intervals

-ful (*suffix*), enough to fill; full of

full′-blown′ (fùl′blōn′), in full bloom

fused sil′i ca (fūzd sil′ə kə), a hard, white or colorless substance appearing as sand, quartz, etc., that has been melted and cooled

g

gal′ax y (gal′ək si), a group of stars or heavenly bodies such as the Milky Way

gal′lant (gal′ənt), brave; determined

---

hat, āge, cãre, fäther; let, ēqual, tèrm; it, īce; hot, ōpen, ôrder; oil; house; cup, fùll, rüle, ūse; th, thin; ᴛʜ, then; zh, measure; ə represents *a* in about, *e* in taken, *i* in pencil, *o* in lemon, *u* in circus

gal′le on (gal′i ən), a large ship used from the fifteenth to the eighteenth centuries

gear (gēr), tools or equipment used for a certain task

ge ol′o gy (ji ol′ə ji), a study of the earth's rocks and minerals

ges′ture (jes′chər), a motion of any part of the body to convey an idea

griz′zled (griz′əld), having gray hair; uncombed gray hair

groove (grüv), a rut or furrow cut by a tool

h

hal′i but (hal′ə bət), a very big flatfish, widely used for food

ha′lo (hā′lō), ring of light around

hard′ship (härd′ship), something hard to bear, such as cold, hunger, etc.

haz′ard (haz′ərd), danger; risk

hear′say′ (hēr′sā′), rumor or gossip that may or may not be based on facts

hem′i sphere (hem′ə sfēr), half of a globe; like a ball cut through the middle

hos til′i ty (hos til′ə ti), resistance; unfriendliness

hov′er (huv′ər), stay near one place

hull (hul), framework of a ship or airplane

hum′ble (hum′bəl), respectful

i

i′dle (ī′dəl), quiet; not moving

ig nore′ (ig nôr′), refuse to notice; pay no attention

il lu′mi nate (i lü′mə nāt), make bright; light up

im- (*prefix*), not; the opposite of

im pede′ (im pēd′), hinder; get in the way of

im pen′e tra ble (im pen′ə trə-bəl), cannot be seen through

in′come (in′kum), that which comes in (usually money) from labor, business, property, etc.

in′fer ence (in′fər əns), a conclusion based on reasoning

in′fi nite ly (in′fə nit li), very greatly; extremely

in′fra red′ (in′frə red′), pertaining to rays that are invisible heat waves

in gen′ious (in jēn′yəs), clever

in quir′y (in kwir′i), question; search for information

in scrip′tion (in skrip′shən), something written on paper, metal, stone, etc.

in sig′ni a (in sig′ni ə), symbol, emblem, or badge indicating rank or office

in′sig nif′i cant (in′sig nif′ə kənt), unimportant; not related

in spire′ (in spir′), encourage

in tent′ (in tent′), listening carefully; concentrating

in ter′pret (in tėr′prit), bring out the meaning of; explain

in volve′ (in volv′), require

-ious (*suffix*), having; full of

ir- (*prefix*), not; the opposite of

-ish (*suffix*), somewhat; like

i′so late (ī′sə lāt), separate from; lonely

j

jour′nal (jėr′nəl), daily record of important events

joust (just), contest between two knights on horseback

jus′tice (jus′tis), fair treatment

jus′ti fy (jus′tə fī), give reason for

just′ly (just′li), fairly

k

key (kē), a low island; a sandy or rocky strip at or near the surface of the water

l

land′mark′ (land′märk′), something to mark a place

lank (langk), slender; thin

lead (lēd), a crack in the ice

Ley′den jar (lī′dən jär), a device for storing electricity

lin′guist (ling′gwist), one who specializes in the study of language

lit′er ar′y (lit′ər er′i), having to do with literature; writing

lit′er a ture (lit′ər ə chür), written works, especially those writings which are known for their beauty and style

loot (lüt), rob

m

main′te nance (mān′tə nəns), those people who check the plane and keep it in good running condition

ma′jor (mā′jər), important

man′kind′ (man′kīnd′), human beings

ma nure′ (ma nür′), animal refuse used to make the land produce more; fertilizer

MATS Mule (mats mūl), nickname given this jet; "Mats" was formed by using the first letters of the words *M*ilitary *A*ir *T*ransport *S*ervice

-ment (*suffix*), act of; state of

mere′ly (mēr′li), only; simply

mi′cro groove′ (mī′krō grüv′), a small groove or rut used on long-playing records

mi′cro scop′ic (mī′krə skop′ik), small; that which can be seen only with a microscope

mi′cro tome (mī′krō tōm), a machine used for slicing microscopic samples for viewing

mil′li me′ter (mil′ə mē′tər), a unit of measure; $\frac{1}{1000}$ of a meter

mir′a cle (mir′ə kəl), a wonderful and unnatural happening

mod′est (mod′ist), not vain; reserved

mu′ti ny (mū′tə ni), revolt against a leader, especially the captain of a ship

---

hat, āge, cãre, fäther; let, ēqual, tėrm; it, īce; hot, ōpen, ôrder; oil; house; cup, fủll, rüle, ūse; th, thin; ᴛʜ, then; zh, measure; ə represents *a* in about, *e* in taken, *i* in pencil, *o* in lemon, *u* in circus

372

mu′tu al (mū′chü əl), done by or for each other

n

N. Lat. (nôrth lat′ə tüd), measurement in degrees north of the equator

nau′se at ed (nô′shi āt əd), sick at the stomach

-ness (*suffix*), state of being

non po′rous (non pô′rəs), without open air spaces; solid

o

ob′li ga′tion (ob′lə gā′shən), responsibility; duty

o′cean og′ra pher (ō′shən og′rə-fər), one who studies ocean life, tides, etc.

oc′to pus (ok′tə pəs), a sea animal with a soft body and eight arms

om′i nous (om′ə nəs), threatening

op′ti cal (op′tə kəl), made to aid sight; visual

or dain′ (ôr dān′), appoint officially; decide; establish as law

out last′ (out last′), last longer than something else

o′ver land′ (ō′vər land′), on the land; over the land

p

pac′i fy (pas′ə fī), keep peace; satisfy

par′al lel (par′ə lel), running in the same direction, such as lines or railroad tracks

par′a phrase (par′ə frāz), keep the same meaning but use different words

parch′ment (pärch′mənt), sheepskin dried, stretched, and cleaned so it can be used like writing paper

ped′es tal (ped′is təl), a supporting stand

pen′du lum (pen′jü ləm), a hanging weight which swings back and forth

pen′e trate (pen′ə trāt), pass into or through

pen′ta gon (pen′tə gon), five-sided figure

Pen′te cost (pen′tə kôst), religious day; the seventh Sunday after Easter

per cent′ (pər sent′), by the hundred; one of a hundred equal parts; $\frac{1}{100}$

per′il (per′əl), danger; risk

pe rim′e ter (pə rim′ə tər), a measure of the distance around a plain surface

pe′ri od (pēr′i əd), a length of time; punctuation mark; unit of three digits in arithmetic

per′ish (per′ish), die

per′ma nent (pėr′mə nənt), lasting; enduring; not temporary

Phar′aoh (fãr′ō), ruler of ancient Egypt

plank′ton (plangk′tən), the tiny animal and plant life that float quietly or swim weakly in a body of water

plaque (plak), a small flat piece of metal or wood

373

plot (plot), to plan secretly; a small piece of land; to mark the location; a sequence of the main parts of a story

por´trait (pôr´trit), a picture or likeness of a person

por tray´ (pôr trā´), describe; show

pot´ash´ (pot´ash´), a wood ash substance used in making glass or soap

pre scribed´ (pri skrībd´), set; specified; designated

pres tige´ (pres tēzh´), glory; recognition; reputation

pre sume´ (pri züm´), suppose

pri´or (prī´ər), earlier

prong (prông), one of the pointed ends of an anchor or a fork

pro´to zo´a (prō´tə zō´ə), tiny one-celled animals, usually found in drops of water

pur sue´ (pər sü´), follow; carry on

q

qual´i fy (kwol´ə fī), modify; change somewhat; limit

quartz (kwôrts), a kind of stone containing crystals

quill (kwil), a pen made from a feather

quin´tu plet (kwin´tü plit), a group of five

qui´pu (kē´pü), an arithmetical counting and recording device used by the ancient Inca Indians of Peru

r

ra´di ant (rā´di ənt), shining; bright

ra´di us (rā´di əs), a straight line from the center to the outer edge of a circle

ram´ble (ram´bəl), to talk or write in a wandering fashion

ra vine´ (rə vēn´), deep valley worn by water

re- (*prefix*), again; back

realm (relm), kingdom; land; field

rec´i pe (res´ə pi), formula; directions

rec´re a´tion (rek´ri ā´shən), amusement; play; pastime

reef (rēf), a rocky or sandy strip at or below the surface of the water

re nown´ (ri noun´), fame; praise

re search´ (ri sėrch´), careful looking for facts or proof

rev´e la´tion (rev´ə lā´shən), something made known

rev´o lu´tion (rev´ə lü´ shən), a circular movement around a point

rid´i cule (rid´ə kūl), make fun of; laugh at in scorn

rime (rīm), a tale written in verse; a rhyme; a verse

route (rüt), way to go

ru´ral (rür´əl), in the country

hat, āge, cãre, fäther; let, ēqual, tèrm; it, īce; hot, ōpen, ôrder; oil; house; cup, fùll, rüle, ūse; th, thin; ҭн, then; zh, measure; ə represents *a* in about, *e* in taken, *i* in pencil, *o* in lemon, *u* in circus

s

sa′ga (sä′gə), story of heroic deeds passed on from one to another, sometimes in rhyme and sometimes set to music

sal′ly (sal′i), ride forth; rush suddenly

sat′el lite (sat′ə līt), a natural or man-made object that revolves around a larger heavenly body

scope (skōp), distance covered; extent

scroll (skrōl), roll of parchment or paper containing written records

scu′ba (skü′bə), a word formed by using the first letters of the words *s*elf-contained *u*nder-water *b*reathing *a*pparatus

scut′tle (skut′əl), to sink a ship by making holes below the water line

scythe (sīтн), a tool for cutting grass or hay

sea′ cu′cum ber (sē′ kū′kum bər), a small sea animal, related to the starfish, that looks something like a cucumber

sen′es chal (sen′ə shəl), manager

sen′si tive (sen′sə tiv), aware; concerned with

sen′try (sen′tri), guard or watchman

se′quence (sē′kwəns), one following another in correct order

se′ries (sēr′iz), sequence; two or more in succession

sex tet′ (seks tet′), group of six

sheathe (shēтн), cover; clothe

shuf′fle (shuf′əl), walk slowly dragging or scraping the feet

sledge′ ham′mer (slej′ ham′ər), a hammer so heavy that it often takes both hands to use it

snipe (snīp), a bird which has a long, narrow bill; something pointed, like a snipe's bill

snor′kel (snôr′kəl), a breathing device for use under water

spec′i men (spes′ə mən), sample; example

spec′u late (spek′ū lāt), consider; think about

speed om′e ter (spēd om′ə tər), an instrument for measuring speed

sphere (sfēr), a ball-shaped object

spin (spin), tell a story with many details

spin′dle neck′ (spin′dəl nek′), a long, thin neck

stand′ard (stan′dərd), flag, emblem, or banner

stan′za (stan′zə), a verse of a poem

stealth′i ly (stel′thə li), in a sneaky way

stim′u late (stim′ū lāt), arouse; encourage

stow′a way′ (stō′ə wā′), a person who hides on a ship, train, etc., to get a free ride

strew (strü), scatter around

strive (strīv), try very hard

sub due′ (səb dü′), overcome; conquer

sub sist′ (səb sist′), remain alive

su′per sti′tion (sü′pər stish′ən), belief without basis; a false fear

surf (serf), sea waves breaking on the shore

sur vey' (sər vā'), look over; examine; measure

sys'tem at'i cal ly (sis'təm at'ik-li), in a planned way

t

tar'nish (tär'nish), to become dull or discolored

tech ni'cian (tek nish'ən), an expert in a special skill

tempt (tempt), persuade; appeal strongly

te re'do (tə rē'dō), a worm-like animal that destroys the wood of ships

ter'mi nal (tėr'mə nəl), a building at either end of a line of transportation

ter rain' (te rān'), ground; piece of land

ther mom'e ter (thər mom'ə tər), an instrument for measuring temperature

ther'mo stat (thėr'mə stat), an automatic device that keeps heat at a fixed or steady temperature

time'-lapse' (tīm'laps'), at spaced intervals

tour'na ment (tėr'nə mənt), contest of skill between two groups of knights on horseback

trans late' (trans lāt'), write in another language

trans mit' (trans mit'), carry over or across

treach'er ous (trech'ər əs), unsafe; not to be trusted

trea'son (trē'zən), acts against the king or the government

trem'u lous (trem'ū ləs), quivering; trembling

trig'ger (trig'ər), set off; start

tum'bler (tum'blər), a water glass

u

un- (*prefix*), not; the opposite of

un'der es'ti mate (un'dər es'tə-māt), to place too low a figure on the size or worth of something

un rav'el (un rav'əl), solve; make plain or clear

ur'ban (ėr'bən), in the city

u'ti lize (ū'tə līz), put to use

v

vain (vān), proud; self-centered

val'iant (val'yənt), brave; noble

vast (vast), great; enormous .

ven'ture some (ven'chər səm), seeking adventure or new experiences; daring

ver'i fy (ver'ə fī), prove to be true; support

ver'ti cal (vėr'tə kəl), straight up and down

vict'uals (vit'əlz), food supplies

vi'sion (vizh'ən), a mental image; sense of sight

---

hat, āge, cãre, fäther; let, ēqual, tėrm; it, īce; hot, ōpen, ôrder; oil; house; cup, fùll, rüle, ūse; th, thin; ᴛʜ, then; zh, measure; ə represents *a* in about, *e* in taken, *i* in pencil, *o* in lemon, *u* in circus

vi′sor (vī′zər), the front part of a cap or helmet which protects the eyes

viv′id (viv′id), clear

volt′me′ter (vōlt′mē′tər), an instrument for measuring voltage of electricity

w

won′drous (wun′drəs), remarkably; unusually

wouldst (wŭdst), a poetic expression meaning "would"

wrench (rench), a tool for holding or turning mechanical parts

y

-y (*suffix*), full of; having; activity

yield (yēld), produce

Word List

The following 978 words are presented in *From Coins to Kings*, Basic Sixth Reader, *Strand 2* of The Harper & Row Basic Reading Program. The word form or the word combination here given is the one in which the word first appears.

11

12

13

14 concentrating
terminal
belly
swept-back

15 vertical
fin
Kratovil
briskly
commenced
maintenance

16 idol

17 population
geography

18 cash
Latin
pendulum
appendix
appendage

19 dawdled
diplomatic
cringe
adversity
impede

20 tumbler
Tex

21 Antarctica
tunnels
trenches
hospital
dining

22

23 graph
rural
urban

24 lamps
errands

25 Slim
rattlers
ledges
intent

26 arid

27

28 Ned
wore
entertain

29 catalogue

30 route
industries

31 recreation

32

33 Panama
Jamaica

34

35 Allen
lungs
scuba
panic
gasped
aqualung

36 coral
currents
reef
flippers
fought
depth

37 throat
suffocating
shoved
mask
Louise
gulped

38 strokes
practically

39

40 napkins
lemonade
beaches
isolated

41 sunken
vessels
colonies
sank
galleon

42 limestone
teredo
chip
visions
jewels
interrupted
reminded

43 sequence

44

45 anticipate
shrimp

46

47 swam
twilight
emerged
crevices
buffeted
strewn

48 gesturing
glided
beckoned
hovering
impatiently
gleaming

49 dagger
shipwreck
capsized
debated

50 anchor
prong
disguised

51 grease
plastic

52

53

54

55 introduced

56 accent

57 argued
bet

58 curtly
suspiciously
mood

59

60 lying
systematically
coral-
encrusted
yielded
diameter

61 ignoring
exclaimed
sledge

62

63 Philippus
Philip
doubloon
looted
silence

64 scary

65 stealthily
   seized
   raging
   scuttled

66

67 stealing

68 tones
   grizzled
   traits
   secretary

69 dictating
   tempted
   inspired

70

71 research
   inference

72 involved

73 oceanographer
   hobby
   blame
   Dr. Marco

74 well-trimmed
   ah
   tales
   anxious

75

76 eliminate
   cargo
   museum

77 corroding
   plaque
   Smithsonian

78 inscription
   nodded
   Santa Anna

79 invaded
   Henry
      Morgan
   although
   knighted
   piracy

80 plotted
   wealthy
   raid
   whew

81 unravel
   exhibits

82 inquiry
   shame
   satisfaction
   humor

83 knit

84 consult

85 compound
   vocabulary

86

87

88 Greek

89

90

91

92

93 Hannu
   Herodotus
   Strabo
   Pliny the
      Elder

94 deserves

95 B.C.
   A.D.
   conflict
   Europe
   ancestors
   translated

96 paraphrase

97 temple
   Somalia
   Hanno
   Punt
   spices
   Pharaoh
   statues

98 Greece
   Minor
   Archipelago
   Dnieper
   incense
   rival

99 Mediterranean
   India
   mounds
   collect
   giant

100 Persians
    Nile
    crocodiles
    tongue

101

102 sphere
    assume

103

104 Italy
    army
    far-fetched
    zones

105 equinox
    occurs
    Arabia

106 monsters

107 various
    Christ

108

109 bulletin
    banner

110 voyages
    altered
    concepts
    Leif Ericson's
    Vinland

111 Norseman
    Canada
    saga

112 sung
    tide
    booths
    salmon

113 vines

114 Marco Polo
    Venice
    Cathay
    prisoner
    Genoa
    parchment

115

116 emperors
    ye
    Peking

117 Kublai Khan
    checkerboard
    justice
    noblemen
    soldiers

118 laughter

119 Christopher
       Columbus
    Indies
    debt
    Portugal

120 cheaper
    Toscanelli
    Lisbon
    geology
    Juan de
       la Cosa

121 obtaining
    influence
    journal
    exalted

122 fleet
    Don
    Palos
    labor
    complained

123 Pinta
    Niña

124 timid

125 Las Casas
    lawyer
    ordained
    published
    Amerigo
       Vespucci
    credit

126

127 Vasco da
       Gama
    superstition
    equatorial
    violent
    doldrums

128 samples
    rewarded

129 hemisphere

130

131 mutiny

132 Balboa
    Haiti
    cask
    victuals
    bold
    courteous
    claimed

133 deed
    pardoned
    treason
    pacifying
    jealous
    death

134 Magellan
    Portuguese
    starvation
    Philippines

135 positive
    diary

136 bargains
    fowls
    scissors

137 penguins
    tame
    paws
    webbed

138 biscuit
    rats
    subdue
    dismay
    musket
    poisoned

139

140 swamps
    empires
    Holland

141 ignorance

142 venturesome
    John Cabot
    Juan Ponce
      de León
    Hernando
      Cortes
    Francisco
      Pizarro
    Jacques
      Cartier
    Martin
      Frobisher
    Samuel de
      Champlain
    René Robert
      de La Salle
    Vitus Bering
    Russia

143

144 public

145 Esther
      Holden
      Averill
    illus.
    Feodor
      Rojankovsky
    Harper &
      Row

146

147

148

149

150 Dutch
    competition

151 Zealand
    Thursday

152 surf
    bay
    Sidney
    beads
    darts

153 swords
    Stingray
    Botany
    peril

154 kangaroo
    mouse-color

155

156 rejected
    scorched
    hostility

157 Lewis
    Clark
    Louisiana
    Territory
    surveyed

158 Montana
    companions
    fork
    warriors

159

160 ravines

161

162 tobacco
    exposure

163 David
      Livingstone
    Henry M.
      Stanley

164 Herald
    boughs
    giraffes

165 Tanganyika
    patience

166 rags
    presume

167 praise
    bade

168 qualifying
    qualification

169 evident

170 Zebulon
      Pike
    George
      Vancouver
    Louis
      Hennepin

171 Sven Hedin
    Sir Richard
      Francis
      Burton
    James
      Bruce

172 twentieth

173 Robert E.
      Peary
    Ellesmere
    Eskimos

174 igloos
    awoke

175

176 dread
    weary

177 absolutely

178 N. Lat.
    auspices
    prestige
    axis
    formally

179 Roald
      Amundsen
    Norwegian
    barrier
    essential
    factor

180 severe
    permanent
    shelters
    carcass

181 adequately
    radius
    gallant

182 Yuri Gagarin
    satellite

183 drank

184 halo
    gradual
    violet
    Balkans
    spherical

185 Jacques
      Piccard
    Swiss
    Don Walsh
    bathyscaph
    Guam

381

293 intended
radically
formula
resolving
electron
electromagnets

294 penetrates
diffuse
fluorescent
emits
optical

295 virus
poliomyelitis

296 obligation

297

298 par.

299 scurry
curb
captivated
activities
sill

300 blurred
focus
millimeters

301 utility
diminished
universe
ample
eclipses
comets

302 Johannes
Kepler
calculating
solar
genius
trial
revelations

303 Andromeda
asteroids
vast

304 Regulus
Leo

305 Sirius

306 Orion's

307 observatories
exquisitely

308 saucer-shaped
Hale
Palomar

309

310

311 comprise
individual
scope

312 concise
vicarious

313

314 Polaroid

315

316 stomach
aerial
taxation

317

318 terrain
fortifications
X-ray
movies
chewed

319 triggered

320 whizzing
revolution

321 time-lapse
crystal
gorgeous

322 weak
infrared
impenetrable
documents
scrolls
Jerusalem

323

324 literature

325 sermon

326 adopted
hyphen
conform

327

328 linguist
etymology
thermostat
groove
microgroove

329

330

331

332 Arthur
strives
distinguish
knighthood

333 Uther
Pendragon
ill
Merlin
kingdom
Ector
Archbishop of
Canterbury
counseled

334 miracle
divinely
marble
anvil
barons
tournament

335 Kay
jousts
sentries
swear
assayed

336 alas
nay
dole
foster
seneschal
twelfth
Pentecost

337 slay
denies
knelt
mercy
thee
altar
crowned
vowed
realm

338 critically
essay

339

340 Chivalry
archers
serfs
peasants
primarily
frequent

341 mutual
pledged
loyalty
armor
lances
wrestle

342 promoted
rank
squire
defense

343 feat
religious
solemn
ceremony
praying

344 blade
proclaimed
Saint
dub
insignia
commissions

345 verify

346 satire
Miguel de
Cervantes
ridicules
Quixote
behave
novel

347

348 stew
pigeon
income
holidays
wits

349 notion
tarnished
scoured
slashed

350 nag
prancing
Rosinante
romantic
steed
absurd
Dulcinea

351 sallied
clad
buckler
terrible
craze

352 visor
rudeness
screamed
threatened
aye
forsooth

353 giggling
valiant
boon
bewilderment
chapel
rescuing
maidens
distress

354 thou
surrender
thy
ominous

355 daze
brink
obey
shuffled

356 vain
humble
modest
ingenious

357 sport
excerpts
adhere
realistic
aspects
emphasize

358 sheathed
blare

359 prescribed
courtesy
opponent
comrade
slain

360 enchantment
Accolon
coward
cruel
punishment
evildoers

361 princess
monks
furiously
terrified

362 portray
falconry

363 excess

364 climax
restored

365

384